Dancing at the Shame Prom

DANCING
at the
SHAME PROM

sharing the stories that kept us small

EDITED BY **AMY FERRIS** & **HOLLYE DEXTER**

SEAL

Dancing at the Shame Prom
Sharing the Stories That Kept Us Small

Copyright © 2012 by Amy Ferris & Hollye Dexter, Editors

Published by
SEAL PRESS
A Member of the Perseus Books Group
1700 Fourth Street
Berkeley, California

Library of Congress Cataloging-in-Publication Data

Dancing at the shame prom : sharing the stories that kept us small / Amy
Ferris and Hollye Dexter, eds.—1st ed.
    p. cm.
    ISBN 978-1-58005-416-4
1. Shame. 2. Sharing. 3. Women—Biography. I. Ferris, Amy Schor. II.
Dexter, Hollye, 1963–
    BF575.S45.D36 2012
    152.4'4—dc23
            2012012284

9 8 7 6 5 4 3 2

Cover design by Elke Barter
Interior design by Kate Basart, Union Pageworks
Printed in the United States of America
Distributed by Publishers Group West

CONTENTS

INTRODUCTION

⋮

"We live in an atmosphere of shame. We are ashamed of everything that is real about us; ashamed of ourselves, of our relatives, of our incomes, of our accents, of our opinions, of our experience, just as we are ashamed of our naked skins."—*George Bernard Shaw*

It's *the big* one—that big, bad, ugly secret we don't want to share.
It keeps us from being intimate, truthful, fearless.
It keeps us *oh, so* small.

It's the sad, funny, joyous, difficult, liberating, humorous, and *holy*
     shit . . . enlightening stories.
It's life-altering.
It's there, in the back of the drawer, hidden next to the sexy lingerie that is
     never, ever worn.
It is a companion, an unwelcome visitor.
It comes at the wrong moment.

A destroyer of dreams, a pervasive darkness; an enabler.
It arrives in the form of anxiety attacks, cold sweats, and sleepless nights.
It has brought down countries, damaged political careers, upended the
     financial world, and shaken religious and spiritual communities.
It is a stoic face in public, a tear-stained face in private.

Aretha sang about it.
Ted Swaggart prayed to almighty God about it.
Elizabeth Edwards wrote and spoke about it.

Angelina Jolie had it tattooed to remind her of it.
Newt Gingrich begged forgiveness because of it.
Tiger Woods lied because of it.
Oprah Winfrey did seventeen shows on it.
Bill Clinton addressed the nation three times in the name of it.
Laura Nyro wrote lyrics about it.
Ruth Madoff lives in hiding because she is filled with it.

The shame we carry from our mothers, our fathers, our siblings, our
    friends, our co-workers. The shame we hide, the shame we pass on to
    our children; the shameful, the shameless. The shame on you and the
    shame on me.

It comes in all colors.
All sizes.
All shapes.
All religions.

It prevents us from loving, giving, sharing, holding, touching, kissing, and
    opening our hearts and souls.

It is felt by men and women and girls and boys, alike.
It does not discriminate.
It is heartbreaking and funny and scary and enlightening and, oh my god, a
    common bond that connects us, just like dots.

The shame of . . . dropping out of school.
Of kissing a girl.
Of kissing a boy.
Of loving the same sex.

Of going to jail.
Of having AIDS or HIV or an STD.
Of loving the wrong skin color.
Of shoplifting.
Of stealing.
Of bankruptcy.
Of lying.
Of wearing briefs, not boxers.
Of having no money.
Losing a job.
Losing your virginity.
Losing your home.
Losing your mind.

The shame of sex.
Drugs.
Small breasts.
And yes, big breasts.

The shame of selling out.
Selling off.
Selling, period.

This anthology is all about sharing/writing our deepest shame, and in the process offering a hand, a shoulder, a box of tissues, tremendous hope, a bit of enlightenment, a bucket of wisdom, and unyielding courage so others who have lived with their own shame realize they, too, have the option to leave it behind, move on, and yes, *yes* . . . let it go.

We want to shatter the stigma of that scary word *shame* and send this message to women (and men) everywhere: You are not alone—we are *right there* with you. In revealing our true stories, we hope you will feel empowered to awaken to your own greatness, to laugh, to share, to lighten up! Yes, we all live with regret and shame, but when we can release and heal it, we become stronger in the places where we were once broken.

In this anthology, we *show* you what it feels like, looks like, tastes like to face that universal nightmare, to strip naked and walk brazenly through school. Twenty-seven gifted writers have agreed to hold hands and plunge into the deep end together, with soul-baring honesty and humor, in the hopes that you, our readers, will follow. We invite you to join us at the Shame Prom—a place where we wear our ugly dresses, then shed them. Where we parade our shame in public, dance it around on our arm, and take awkward pictures with it. But afterward, we're not going to roll around in the backseat making out with it. This time, we're breaking up with Shame and driving off into the sunset, stronger in knowing that we are connected at the deepest, most human level.

So put on your tiaras, people. Let's get this party started.

Welcome to the Shame Prom
where everyone is invited to dance.

—Amy Ferris and Hollye Dexter

THREAD BY THREAD
Lyena Strelkoff

:

There is a woman on a stage. You see her body in graceful silhouette against a rich purple screen. Her arms unbuckle and arch, like wings unfurling. She sways and spins. As she dances, she tells a story about a caterpillar emerging from its cocoon. It is a true story, her story. It is shocking, painful, moving, and beautiful. She is laughing, luminous. She is sitting in a wheelchair.

She tells this story on stages across America, and speaks to thousands about her life. Critics call her a "master storyteller." Audiences return again and again. Her stories are transformational.

By most accounts, this woman's life is wonderful. She has, for a decade, been in deep love with a husband who adores her. She has a beautiful baby boy, whom she is thrilled and honored to mother. She is admired by many, loved by dear friends, and well supported by her family. She manages her significant disability mostly with grace, and lives a joyful, fulfilling life.

This woman is me. But, sometimes, I don't recognize her. It's as if my life belongs to someone else, another me, who is brave and brilliant and shining. Not the deeply flawed, intensely lonely person I have known myself to be.

When I was three, my parents separated. Pulling his three daughters off his body, one crying child at a time, my father left. I can't say I exactly remember it, but I have an image in my mind. My horror-stricken mother. My glum, resolute father. My sisters and I, sad, scared, and bawling. For the next few years, my parents waged a quiet custody battle, civil and private, but ultimately dangerous. Its defining event was an attempt by my father to take us without my mother's knowledge. I remember being alone in his car, "Stay here!" my father barking, my sister running up the street, shouts from inside the house, a policeman peeking in the car window, watching, from the upstairs landing, as they handcuffed my father.

When it was over, this moment of colossal poor judgment and catastrophic insensitivity had demolished most of what was left of the family I knew. Nearly every relationship had been altered, some entirely wrecked. In a single afternoon, the unstable foundation on which I'd been standing crumbled heavily, violently into a heap.

It was devastating for each of us in our own way, but for me, the youngest of our clan, it was obliterating. When I think of it, a frozen numbness overtakes me, like an alpine meadow after an avalanche, eerily still, with no sign of the life that once flourished there. Because I was so young, there was nowhere to place myself except at the center of events. I understood it the only way I could: It was my fault.

In the rough sketches of memory, I see my mother in bed, looking too small. I see her fumbling with her hair as I wait, again, for her to take me to school. I see her chopping vegetables and crying. When I ask her about it, she wipes her eyes and says it's onions. I start crying, too.

I see my sister dividing our room with a long piece of yarn. I see myself in bed in the dark, anxiously rubbing the rough edge of my coverlet. I don't see my oldest sister.

My father was granted regular visitation at his home four hundred miles from ours. But my oldest sister was busy with her teenage life and my other sister refused to see him. I remember lying in the canopy bed he'd bought me, staring at my sister's yellow headboard above her empty bed. I remember my sister making me swear I wouldn't tell him where she was. I remember crying to go home. I remember getting sick. I remember my father, acting like everything was fine.

❀

I emerged from those years scarred by a deep sense of insecurity and a deeper sense of inadequacy. Clearly, something was wrong with me. Clearly, I was bad or broken. Why else would these things happen? Why else would my family change? I was deeply ashamed of my imperfection, my insufficiency. I was ashamed of what I perceived to be my inherent flawedness, like an ugly, creeping bruise inside me.

And so the campaign began, the unconscious drive to hide the mess inside. I didn't know what that mess was, exactly. I just knew I had to bury it. Maybe then people wouldn't leave. Maybe then bad things would stop happening. I could be happy. I could go home.

I hid mostly behind my competencies. And, to a large degree, it worked. Ask anyone who knew me and they'll remember a pretty girl— confident, mature, talented, smart. They'll remember that I was kind and compassionate. They'll remember that I was popular and admired. But all this goodness came at a price. By the time I was in eighth grade, I'd long lost the ability to genuinely connect with my peers, afraid of any kind of intimacy. Being close would surely reveal how flawed I was, and bad things would certainly follow.

By the time I graduated high school, shame left me utterly alone. I remember wandering the halls at lunch, pretending I had somewhere to go, because I didn't have anyone I could sit with. I still had a lot of "friends" and I was still well regarded, but the loneliness of self-imposed isolation was slowly crushing me.

College brought a small ray of hope when I finally landed in therapy. There, I slowly began to recognize the sea of shame in which I'd been swimming. Prior to that, I was like a fish, unaware of the water that's always been home. I began to see my issues—crippling perfectionism, fear of intimacy, obsession with my weight—as symptoms of that shame. And I started to realize that shame, like a massive, impenetrable coat, was keeping me from the close friendships I craved. It was the source of my perpetual loneliness, and I'd have to shed it if I wanted things to change.

Thread by thread, I started to pick at it.

Over the next ten years, as I pursued a career in acting and dance, I flexed my authenticity muscle. I confronted my father, insisting that our relationship include my story. He rose to the occasion beautifully, acknowledging my pain and apologizing for the role he'd played in it. I created short performance pieces that blended my personal stories with movement, art, and poetry. Off-stage, I spoke my truth more often than not, messy and inconvenient as it might be, and let myself actually be seen. It was a constant, flawed practice, a fail-and-try-again practice. It was awkward, uncomfortable, and scary. As the muscle grew, shame began to shrink around some issues, and even disappear.

But the greatest test was still to come.

In my early thirties, I started dating Dean. Our friendship was fierce and complicated, and quickly grew passionate. One Friday morning, making love in the olive light of his bedroom, I was overcome by the perfect orgasm. It was soulful and sublime. I surrendered totally, letting it envelop me.

When it was over, I couldn't lie still. Dean wanted to snuggle in the quiet calm, but I was up and moving. I didn't know why, couldn't stop to think about why. I just had to keep moving.

We went for a hike on a trail overlooking the ocean. I asked Dean questions to get him talking, just so I could focus on my own thoughts. Was this really the man I wanted to be with? Would this relationship work? The orgasm had been consuming, *obliterating*, even. Would this be another avalanche?

I was frantic with anxiety. I couldn't calm my mind, couldn't quiet the constant questioning. I didn't realize it, but the deep connection of our lovemaking had scared me near to death.

From the trail, I saw a beautiful oak tree. I'd always climbed trees, found solace in trees. I started to climb, scrambling both away from my fear and toward reliable comfort. But even in the branches, I didn't feel better. The cool bark under my palms, my sure feet deftly finding each hold, nothing helped. So I climbed higher. When relief continued to elude me, I looked for a better perch.

Twenty feet up, I stopped to listen to a joke Dean was telling. I was uncomfortable, antsy, but standing still. And then a branch broke.

I realized instantly what was happening. I reached in front of me for something to grab, something to anchor this moment and keep it from evolving into the next. But it was no use. Gravity pulled me from the tree.

Like my father pulling me from his body, the fall was a threshold. My life was about to change. And I suddenly realized I had a choice. I could flail and fight, trying to wrestle my way out like I'd been wrestling all morning to avoid the growing intimacy with Dean. Or I could surrender and take my chances with life on the other side. It was a familiar cross-roads. Every moment of my life before had held the same two paths. And every moment, I'd struggled to choose the one that led to peace.

This time, the choice was easy. Nothing was going to keep me from hitting the ground. So I relaxed. And gravity stopped pulling.

I floated in the air, feeling euphoric. Time began to crawl like it was moving through honey. I noticed the leaves around me, the shape of my body. I was suspended in that same honey, and the light from where I hung was golden. This is what it felt like to let go. This was the promise of presence and surrender. It was a vivid, joyous connection to God, for She was the honey and this was the ultimate intimacy.

And then, the Earth and I collided. The impact crushed my spinal cord and I was instantly paralyzed from the waist down.

The loss was catastrophic.

I couldn't move, couldn't pee, could barely sit up. My sexual sensation was gone. What had been the best orgasm of my life was now likely to be my last. It was a shock like nothing else I could imagine.

The physical stillness was maddening. I'd danced all my life. Movement was my primary means of self-expression. It was church and therapy. It was one place I could always be authentic. Now it was gone, at least as I had always known it. I turned to writing, in desperate need.

I spent two months in the hospital learning how to manage paralysis, battling infection, and trying to skirt both panic and dread. My journal was a loving friend, tenderly holding my tortured truth.

When I got out, disability made me simultaneously far more and far less visible. A man stepped into an elevator with me, gave me a once-over and said, "So what happened to you?" I was stunned. If I'd been standing, he'd have barely noticed me. And yet, *all* he noticed was the chair. I wanted to say, "What happened to me isn't the most interesting thing about me. Ask what I love about life. Ask what lights me up." But I was so shocked, all I could do was stammer something about having fallen.

Pervasive misconception about life in a chair was plentiful. Some friends expected too much of me. Others, too little. Some people assumed I would heal as if from a badly broken leg. Others thought my life must now be over.

Pity and sympathy were such a waste. I'd been held in the hand of God. Her light was cast on everything now. I saw beauty everywhere, *felt* beauty everywhere. I was happier and more alive than I had ever been.

But it was also grossly hard. Moving from the kitchen to the bedroom across the carpet with a cup of tea was like slogging through tar with my arms and legs bound. Getting dressed exhausted me. And the medical maze was overwhelming, trying to find the right providers, drugs, and therapies to maximize my life.

Most people just couldn't imagine what it was really like. They simply had no way of knowing. And their view of me was inaccurate and incomplete.

It left me aching. Time with friends felt lonely and empty. It was sickeningly familiar. And it was unacceptable.

Managing paralysis was hard enough, but becoming invisible to the people I loved was unbearable. I'd endured that hell for twenty years before, spent ten years clawing my way out. I wasn't about to let even catastrophic disability isolate me again.

I turned to the tools of my trade. I started crafting a performance, a simple offering of true stories that captured the complicated reality of my life with a spinal cord injury. I had two intentions: tell the truth and create something beautiful. It was a tall order.

I wanted people to understand the physical ramifications of my injury—exactly what I could and couldn't do. I wanted to share the extraordinary spiritual awakening it was causing. I wanted to share the humor, the unlikely but plentiful laughs I had. And I wanted to share the pain. In short, I wanted to be seen. Loss had placed me on a transformational journey full of warts and wonder both, and I didn't want to travel alone. It was too hard and too delicious not to share. I'd already learned my lesson. Silence breeds shame, and I refused to feel ashamed of something I had no control over. Clearly, I'd come a long way.

My compulsion was so fierce I didn't think much about what I was doing. I didn't think about potential consequences or the magnitude of risk. I just wrote, and pulled together stories from my hospital journal. I put those stories into a loose order and invited friends and family to a single performance. For two hours, I held their hands as we trekked somewhat sloppily through my disability experience.

When it was over, I felt elated, expansive. *This* was breathing.

A few weeks later, when I sat down to watch the video footage, I was dumbstruck. Something magical had happened in the theater. The audience had been transformed. My story had moved them in ways I didn't anticipate, and far more deeply than I ever hoped. And the woman I saw on stage was glowing. She was vibrant, overflowing with life. Never before had I experienced myself like that. The woman on stage was home.

A year and a half later, I opened a polished version of that first performance, a one-woman play called *Caterpillar Soup*. We planned to run for three weekends, but didn't end up closing until six months later. Critical praise was abundant, but audience response was astounding. People came back three or four times to see the show. They sent me cards and gifts. They wrote me long letters. And the theme was always the same: immense gratitude.

Telling my story in intimate, artful detail had allowed people to see not only me but themselves in honest, compassionate light. It let them acknowledge their fears and own their strength. And for some, it let them release, if only for a moment, their shame. People with no disability experience, whose personal stories were very different from my own, found courage, hope, and inspiration in my journey made transparent. And the effect was deeply healing. For all of us.

Soon the show was touring theaters nationally, and I was being invited to speak at universities around the country. Where once I couldn't connect with a single friend, now I made my living authentically connecting with thousands.

And Dean? The accident we shared brought us ever closer. For two years, I challenged him to leave, still afraid of what being close to him could mean. Love, relationship, family. . . . That's where *real* injury can happen. I pushed him so I'd be sure he was staying for the right reasons. But he refused to budge. And eventually, he loved me into loving him. We married on New Year's Eve, 2006, in the company of one hundred friends, an evening bursting with romance, laughter, and love. And four years later, we were blessed with a beautiful baby boy.

I wish I could stop right here, let this essay end on the high. But if I did, the point of it would be lost. So, I'll tell you this: Despite my accomplishments and the generous admiration of others, I still frequently feel inadequate. I have trouble seeing myself as others see me. I still suffer hindering insecurity, and I still feel, more often than I want to admit, fundamentally flawed. And every time I do, I feel ashamed. Ashamed that I still feel that way. Ashamed that, sometimes, I still believe it.

Perhaps that's the power of shame bred in childhood, when synapses are rapidly forming and the psyche is so impressionable. But the remedy is always the same. Tell the truth. No matter how much I want to hide. No matter how dangerous it feels. I have to flex my authenticity. Because when I do, even while sweating, sure that no one will understand, that this time people will surely abandon me or lose respect for me, three critical (and glorious) things happen. Shame is robbed of threads to build its smothering coat. I am afforded the healing of genuine connection. And others are given permission to hold themselves a little more gently, perhaps to thin the coat they've worn too long, the coat that stifles them.

The truth is a very big place, maddening and marvelous. And the joyous life I live depends on it. It depends on meaningful connection made possible only by embracing the wholeness of me, and letting her be seen. Only then can I truly be free. Only then can I shine.

WHAT *Lyena* HOPES READERS WILL TAKE AWAY FROM HER STORY

"My hope is that readers gain greater compassion for themselves and perhaps a bit of courage to risk letting themselves be truly seen."

THE CICADA KILLER
Teresa Stack

When I was ten years old, I had a bug collection. As a young girl, I thought it was a perfectly reasonable hobby. As I grew older and watched most every person I knew recoil before a daddy longlegs, my appreciation of the insect world began to seem more unique.

Everything can be traced back to my father. Dad was a distant, troubled man who had little use for children. He was often angry, especially when buoyed by his lifelong love affair with Scotch. His alcoholic moods charted our family's daily life, and few things besides an unfiltered cigarette and a strong J&B on the rocks seemed to bring him much pleasure. But he did have an infectious passion for the beauty and wonder of the natural world. He could name all the birds in our yard. He could mimic their songs. We had a robust vegetable garden and a lawn full of flowers. During interludes of sobriety, he taught me to fish for perch and bluegills on nearby lakes, to scout the local woods for edible berries and mushrooms, and, one memorable summer, to collect and identify the bugs that lived near our house in Pittsburgh.

The first thing a serious bug collector needs is a bug-killing container. Mine was a simple glass applesauce jar, with cotton balls soaked in turpentine layered in the bottom (Dad was a patent-holding chemist and designed my system). The fumes in the tightly sealed contraption quickly killed the luckless insects. There was a large flat piece of styrofoam for mounting my bugs, and each night I would sit in my room and identify and label that day's catches. With great care, I would impale each bug using straight pins from Mom's sewing box. Because dead bugs are fragile creatures, careless mounting could damage a precious specimen, breaking a delicate wing or brittle antennae. Precision was paramount.

Every day that summer, I hunted for bugs. It's a solitary, absorbing activity, and that was what I needed. Because my father was so unpredictable, his moods so isolating, we did not have visitors or play with friends at our house. My dad might just as easily dazzle the neighborhood kids with his repertoire of magic tricks as fly into a rage and try to strangle my mother. We kept to ourselves. When the doorbell rang unexpectedly, we all panicked, worried that our crazy world would be exposed. And we made excuses for the screaming, the door slamming, for my father staggering and weaving his way up our street every night, and for the occasional presence of the police.

The coral rose bushes in the front yard were a reliable source of striped potato bugs and metallic Japanese beetles. The uncut fields bordering the county park were jumping with mean-spirited grasshoppers. Hairy wolf spiders hid under the porch, tent worms and woolly bears clung to cherry tree bark, crickets and lightning bugs were ubiquitous. I was busy.

Collecting bugs can be hard work for a kid. What kept me going was the interest my father took in my project. He was genuinely attentive in a way that I had never experienced. Every evening, I waited at the end of our street for him to ascend the rickety wooden stairs that led to the old trolley, as he returned from his salesman's job in the city. On the way home, I'd breathlessly recount my adventures, and he'd promise to look at my new bugs as soon as he'd changed out of his suit. This was remarkably high status in my house.

Every night, as he surveyed my day's insect hunt, he shared new stories of his own youth in semirural Ohio. He told me of the bugs in his boyhood collection, of those he'd particularly admired or feared. He'd once held a live female praying mantis perched on his finger, feeding it raw hamburger from a spoon. He spoke with respect of the brown recluse spider, an unremarkable and timid arachnid fond of hiding in closets and whose powerful venom could bring down a grown man. But his true awe was reserved for a fearsome bug he'd encountered only once, while in the Air Force stationed in New Mexico. I remember the first time I heard the monster's name, sitting at the kitchen table with my dad on a cool June evening: the Cicada Killer.

The Cicada Killer is a giant wasp that preys on cicadas, those thumb-sized, melodious bugs who perform the rhythmic concerts of late summer nights. The black and yellow Killer grows to two inches long, with a massive stinger that contains a powerful neurotoxin. This brutish bug is merciless. The doomed cicadas are stung and effectively immobilized, then dragged back to the underground nest of the Killer. The cicada would remain in the nest, paralyzed, until the Killer's young hatched and proceeded to eat it alive. To an adult man, the sting of the Cicada

Killer felt like being shot with a rifle at close range. So said my dad. I was instantly fascinated by this fiend.

As my bug collection grew that summer, my mounting board became crowded with specimens. One sparkling August afternoon, after returning from a walk to the dairy, I sat on our steps, languidly eating an ice cream sandwich. Suddenly, a loud buzz caught my attention. From the corner of my eye I saw something drop to the ground from a small maple tree about ten feet away. I grabbed the paper bag from the ice cream and crept quickly to the tree. There, in the grass, was something large, squirming. I placed my bag over the wiggly mass and ran to the house for my bug-killing jar.

Returning, winded and with jar in hand, I deftly removed the bag and replaced it with the killing jar, turned upside down on the grass. After all movement in the jar had stopped, I turned the jar upright and secured the lid. To my delight I saw not one but two bugs, truly a collecting coup. One I recognized immediately as an adult cicada. The other appeared to be an exceptionally large wasp.

My anticipation that evening was barely containable. As my father sat down at the kitchen table for the customary evening inspection, I handed him my jar. He looked closely, chuckled to himself while shaking his head, and said, "I'll be damned. You got yourself a Cicada Killer." He'd never seen one in the Northeast, and his pride was palpable. It was, and I believe still is, my finest moment.

I mounted my Killer with great care and gave her center billing on the styrofoam. For a week, no one was safe from my tale of triumph over the sinister and dangerous insect. This was surely the zenith of my bug career.

A few days later, in the middle of a humid night of fitful sleep, I half awoke to the unmistakable sound of an angry insect in my room. Immediately convinced the Killer had come alive to seek her revenge, I tumbled quickly out of bed. Grabbing the styrofoam board, I ran from the bedroom, holding it at arm's length. Opening the front door, I flung the board, like a Frisbee, with all my might. I staggered back to sleep.

In the fuzzy sunshine of the morning, I was horrified at what I had done. Dressing fast, I went with dread to the front yard, hoping my memory was just a nightmare. Sure enough, twenty feet from the door lay my bug collection, upside down. Turning over the styrofoam, I saw that my Cicada Killer had broken off at the abdomen (which was nowhere to be found). She was now no more than half a bug. In the upper-right corner of the board, a small cricket I had mounted the day before rubbed its forelegs together, making cricket noises that I had mistaken for my vengeful Killer. I learned the hard way that certain bugs require extra killing.

That evening I could not bring myself to face my dad. My punky younger brother gleefully told him what had happened. My brother said he laughed.

The episode marked the end of my bug collecting. After the cowardly loss of my trophy, I felt I could not start over. The distance between my father and I returned, at least to my mind. I was overnight turned back from the brave huntress to the frightened child, from the respected daughter to the foolish girl.

✺

Life in our family got harder over the years. Alcoholism is a progressive disease and the insanity escalated. My father's job was in jeopardy; his health deteriorated. It was a scary time. We asked relatives to store our kitchen knives and to hide the bullets from my father's hunting rifles, terrified of my father's inexplicable storms of anger. My brother and I retreated into our own worlds, trying to keep the super-low profile that might avoid our father's attention. As we entered high school, our social isolation only grew. My stoic, long-suffering mother tried every day to keep us together and to keep up the appearance of a normal family. My brother and I both left home as soon as we turned eighteen. (My father bought me suitcases that Christmas to help speed my exit.)

Years later in my midtwenties, I was fishing with my roommate Lisa on a crooked wooden pier in Cape Hatteras, North Carolina. It was a uniquely still night, and Lisa and I were chatting with a white-haired fishing elder, whose deep laugh lines gave him an empathic charm. He seemed taken with the idea of two young women fishing alone on a pier. While recounting for our new friend how I had come to appreciate nature (and learned to fish), I shared my story of the Cicada Killer.

Two weeks later, at home in New Jersey, I received a small brown box in the mail. Wading through several layers of thick cotton, I finally reached a tiny wax paper pouch. Beside it was a note: "I thought that what you needed in your life was another Cicada Killer." Inside the pouch was a bug, dehydrated and not nearly as sinister-looking as in my memory. It seems the old gentleman from Cape Hatteras had an entomologist brother-in-law, who had called around and found this laboratory specimen. It was such perfect closure, too good to be true. I planned to have the Killer professionally mounted in a glass display box.

My father and I had long since grown deeply estranged. Over the years, his anger, his physical violence, and his volatility had gotten worse, and my brother and I kept our distance, staying away for over ten years at a time. But that day I called him, certain this story would offer a brief connection.

To my surprise, he didn't remember my Cicada Killer. I never mounted my new bug.

I think it was the last time my father ever disappointed me, as disappointment requires expectations. I needed to find a way to live without that craziness, to jettison the shaming isolation of all those years and to build a life connected to *other* people. I like to think I also started to forgive him. I imagine it had to do with finally seeing him for who he was and not through the heated wishes of a child.

❋

I'm in my forties now. My father died last year. At seventy-eight, his tortured heart was 100 percent blocked and emergency surgery couldn't save him. Everyone was surprised he lived as long as he did. My mother had stayed with him all these years—a point of pride for her and her generation, I think, and a frustrating puzzle to my peers and me.

Planning his funeral was hard. My mother wanted a funeral "like everyone has": two viewings at the nice funeral parlor in town, a service with a Catholic priest, a luncheon for guests after the interring at the local military cemetery. I wanted to be supportive, but our family was not "like everyone." My parents had no friends that I knew of. My brother and I lived far away. What nice things would we say in the newspaper obituary? Who would come to the funeral parlor? Who would come to a restaurant luncheon my mother insisted on reserving for *twenty people*? I felt years of shame culminating in the already stressful days following his death. A funeral with no people: a final send-off of shame.

But I shepherded the American death protocol for my mother: I ordered the flowers, picked a casket, chose a prayer card, for god's sake. I wrote a respectful obituary my mother could approve of without using the words "loving husband and father," which felt like writing a sentence without vowels. And no one would show up for the funeral. And my brother and my mother and I would be sad and we would cry, not because my father was gone, but for all that should have been.

The morning of the viewing, we dutifully arrived on time and took our assigned places in the parlor. We sat quietly, and we waited. We had decided to close the casket, my father's corpse grotesquely, unrecognizably embalmed.

After a few minutes, two women entered—both neighbors and friends of my mother. Then a few more arrived. Then more. Every time someone entered the room, my mother sighed, gratefully. Our family lived on a large cul-de-sac, had for over forty years. It seemed like almost every neighbor came that day.

At the evening viewing, I was shocked to see that several of my friends from New York and Washington, D.C., had made the long drive for his funeral. And more people came—*friends* he had apparently made in his later, more mellow years, mostly folks he had met at the local restaurant he and my mother patronized three times a week. The bartender, a flirty blond woman, was *crying*. My brother's friends whom he hadn't seen in twenty years, old pals from our neighborhood, came from fifty miles away to pay their respects.

The funeral the next day, at the new military cemetery outside Pittsburgh, was moving. A young airman handed my mother a perfectly folded American flag, and on bended knee, looked her in the eyes and said, "Your country sincerely thanks your husband for his service."

At the luncheon, we filled those twenty spots. We reminisced, not so much about my father, but about growing up together on our Pittsburgh street and where our lives were now. My mother seemed pleased. And I did not feel ashamed.

❋

I still do not know how to mourn my father. He was such a complex man, and not all people who die leave the same kind of grief in their wake. But he had passed on to me and my brother so much of his knowledge, fueling passions that to this day are the most rewarding parts of our lives. And with his death, I learned that my family was more than my father and his demons, and that my father was more than his alcoholism. And I hope that knowledge will help me learn how to say goodbye.

WHAT *Teresa* HOPES READERS WILL TAKE AWAY FROM HER STORY

"I hope that my story conveys a complex relationship with a difficult human being and shows how so much shame lives inside our heads (and not in the real world). I also dream that readers will come away with a new openness about how very cool insects can be."

YEAR OF THE RAT
Nina Burleigh

⋮

It was 1980, disco to punk, Carter to Reagan. I was a potty-mouthed, semi-alcoholic nihilist English major living in a "small Midwestern town" attending a "small Midwestern liberal arts college." There wasn't much to do in that town, which in summer was totally invisible from a distance because of the miles of lush Cargill-operated cornfields around it. The other nine months of the year, when the blanket of perma-cloud blew away, you could see the weather coming from the west for miles and miles. Tornadoes ripped it up regularly. It was that flat.

In my years there, I liked to drink Busch beer and smoke packs of Merits, dabbled in the occasional joint, and thought of myself as literary.

At the time of which I write, I also had a redheaded boyfriend who put blotter acid on his blue eyeball and let it dissolve, when the moon was full.

I thought of myself as a budding writer, but none of the notebooks I scribbled in ever amounted to anything. I was good at penning occasional screeds about Ronald Reagan for the college newspaper. I got in the habit of writing them late at night and submitting them and then sort of hiding out, waiting for the reaction. Born in the Year of the Rat, I was already by nature a furtive creature.

The town had a cultural life, of sorts, consisting of our kooky gay college theater crowd, and with that, a kinky underbelly. I lived on a coed dorm floor where most of the men were gay. One of them kept a trunk by his bed with fisting porn magazines in it. I hung out with this arty crowd, and one of my running buddies was a guy named Josh, slight and greasy, whose father was a local judge and who, therefore, in my mind, had some class cachet. He also had enough family money to own some high-end photo gear. I think he talked about wanting to be a photographer, but mostly we just got drunk on Busch beer at the town bar, and had what we thought of as high-minded literary conversations about Thomas Pynchon and *The Confederacy of Dunces*.

One night, Josh invited me and my blotter-eyed boyfriend to the opening of a photography show of a local man, who he had assisted in producing what they were calling *solar prints*—many of which were black-and-white female silhouettes. You couldn't really see the details, just the outlines of their bodies and faces. One of the models was there, a sporty, clean-cut, pretty girl from the swim team. Josh introduced me to the photographer, whose name was Woody. He had a stubbly, brown beard—that's all I remember. Woody talked about the "process" and the swim team model stood by, not saying much that I remember. I feel like he probably used the word "classy" at some point, but he really had me when he said I had a "European" look. I agreed on the spot to pose for more of his solar prints.

Backing up about seven years: I became a mirror-gazing narcissist around the age of thirteen. Before that, I spent very little time looking at my face; in fact, I had a neurotic phobia of mirrors. I could barely stand the sight of my face as a kid. I didn't feel like that person in the mirror was me at all. In seventh grade, all that fell away and with the awesome precision of hormonal clockwork, I fell in love with my female beauty. My best friend and I started buying teen girl magazines and following instructions for egg-white hair conditioning and mayonnaise facials. I started looking long into the mirror and noticing the curve of my upper lip, and how that redheaded boy with the raspy voice in honors math might just want to kiss me.

When I was fourteen, I decided I was pretty enough to be a model. I think people must have been telling me I was pretty enough to do it, and I believed them. I talked my father into introducing me to a professional photographer he knew, who took pictures of me in my dresses and even a bikini. Those prints are still around in one of my parents' drawers somewhere. I might have sent the prints to Mademoiselle or an agency, but I went nowhere in that field. I was too short and I had no talent with the camera.

Still, the addiction to being gazed at only grew stronger.

Soon enough, big, blushing crushes led to teenage outings clad in slutty Qiana halter dresses, kisses in cars, make-outs on beds, and actual sex to the sound of Pink Floyd on a couch in the basement of my senior year boyfriend's parents' house.

I came right away. No problems with sex—then, or now.

I mention this because the story I am about to share as one of my "shames" is not at all unusual for women, but it's one that falls into the larger category of sexual victimization, a spectrum from poor self-esteem, sexual dysfunction, abuse, and date rape all the way to self-cutting and eating disorders. None of that ever happened to me. When I think back on my misspent youth, I still feel a hint of pride that I had a rat's animal sense of danger about bad people. I was fortunate to have eluded the really nasty things that happened to girls out after dark. I was out after dark all the time, rarely in full control of my faculties, but that animal paranoia was too strong to be snuffed out by the drugs and alcohol I consumed.

A nocturnal animal, I was captured by daylight.

✹

Woody had me at "European." That was about the best thing a girl trapped in a third-rate teachers college in an Illinois cow town could hear. Josh arranged the date and some weeks later, I accompanied him to Woody's chilly studio.

I remember taking off my clothes. I remember starting out sitting on a chair and I remember feeling cold. I remember Josh standing by, holding the lightbox and Woody clicking away. Those were the days of film, so there must have been some minutes passing when I was sitting there in the chair naked and cold, and I think I had a sweater on during those minutes.

My flesh looked white and goosey—it was one of the dead months, November or February. I hardly had the sheen I imagined would be added by the solar prints.

My body resisted the moves Woody wanted from me, in the chair. But what was going on in my mind? That's the hard part. Because now when I think back on it, I can only remember the body.

And here's what the body did.

Woody suggested that I get off the chair and lie on the ground, in a fetal position. My body wanted this, because it was warm. And Woody said if I would just curl up a little more into a ball, that would be even better, because it would work perfectly for what he was calling his "egg" series.

I curved into a ball. That felt even better. I think I had my eyes shut.

Soon, Woody and Josh were working away with camera and light box, down at the lower end of my egg shape. Snap, snap, snap. I remained that way, until they were finished. He reloaded many times.

Then I put my clothes on, and Josh walked me back to the dingy town bar, and bought me a Busch beer. We didn't speak for a while, or if we did, it was awkward. After a beer or two, he announced, quietly, "Pornography's not a bad thing, except for what it does to the people in it."

I pretended not to hear him. But just like that, I snapped awake. Pornography. That's what I had just posed for. There was the burning physical fact of the word. Pornography.

I remember insisting that Woody sign a document saying he wouldn't distribute the prints. And he did that. He pretended to be hurt that I wouldn't let him display what would be beautiful solar prints of my European body. I didn't ask him for the film. I wasn't capable of that sort of challenge. Not then and maybe not now. In any case, it was clear that he had already done what he was going to do with the copies. That trunkful of gay porn in the dorm had its counterparts.

I blocked it out and moved on. I didn't see so much of Josh after that. My blotter-headed boyfriend and I broke up. My parents drove down and watched me graduate. They were about to be divorced and their misery blinded them to everything else. We went to the bar and had a beer, and when we walked back into the parking lot to get into their rust-flecked Chevy, some of the townie guys, the ones who hung out with the guys who tended bar, threw pennies at us.

Four years later, I was twenty-four years old and working at a newspaper in a nearby town. One of my platonic male college friends dropped in for a visit one night. We sat in my apartment living room, drinking beer and smoking pot and rehashing old times. And at some point, he asked me about the naked pictures. He said he'd been in the college town bar one night and some guys he didn't know had brought in naked pictures of me and tried to sell them.

I denied having anything to do with it. Not me, I said, no way.

And he said, he was sure it was me, that I had been sitting in a chair. "Your hair," he said, "it was thrown back over the chair, and you had your back arched."

We talked a bit longer and smoked some more pot. I went into the bathroom and looked in the mirror. An awful pair of dark eyes gazed back at me, framed by long waist-length hair.

Me. Not me. Me. Not me.

I could do nothing about the eyes. But the hair, that I could deal with.

I went into the bedroom and fetched a pair of scissors. I came back and stood before the bathroom mirror and started snipping away.

When I came out, my hair was two inches long. My friend nearly fell off the couch. I don't believe he ever connected his story and my self-barbering.

Some years later, when I was making a name for myself in the business of journalism and writing, it occurred to me that Woody could probably make even more money off those pictures, or embarrass me in some way. Josh, too. I asked around and heard that Josh had become an evangelical Christian. Neutralized.

Woody, I heard, had left the college town with his family (he had a wife and kids, even during his early photo career) and moved to

Ohio to start a goat farm. I considered tracking him down, but there seemed little purpose to it. The cat was out of the bag, my asshole sold on film years ago. It might even have contributed a little bit to his pastoral haven.

I realize that this little episode seems quaint and antique in the era of sexting, when teenage girls email their privates to boyfriends, and sex tapes making the rounds on the Internet are mere badges of celebrity. Certainly whatever remains of my ass on film is decaying in Woody's archive, if he bothered to keep it at all. Assuming the prints got circulated, they, too, must be decayed, cracked. If they made it into print, those magazines are gone, replaced by fresher, more colorful material.

Since then, I have not steered clear of photographers—on the contrary, I married one. He hasn't taken too many naked pictures of me.

I have had very few experiences that replicate that utter replacement of mind with body that I felt as a model for Woody's "egg" series. Giving birth. Maybe dying is like that, too.

In the years since, I probably appear to have been a swashbuckling actor in the big bad world. I travel and make my way alone, and my friends and family think I'm pretty intrepid.

The truth is somewhat different. For one thing, journalism is a passive profession. We stand around and watch people who really do things, and ask questions and wait for their answers. I do carry that little voice in my head telling me not to act, not to DO. Sometimes it's louder and more insistent than other times.

Right now, sitting in a Cairo hotel, eighteen floors above Tahrir Square on Friday the thirteenth, 2012, at 3:00 PM, after Muslim prayers, the sun shining on a cold afternoon, I am here to research what I intend to be a screed about the way conservative Islamists force women to cover themselves in public.

When I do go outside, I find myself feeling terribly exposed among the scarf-headed women, even though I swaddle myself in black layers. The outline of my body is still visible, and the exposed top of my head brings glares or leers from certain men. American slut, they mutter in Arabic. Whore. Fuck me.

When I can, I embrace the furtive, retreat inside my hotel room, send messages online, pull the drapes. I know this isn't the image that I project, nor is it one that I myself always acknowledge. I fight it back, and suppress it totally on most days. But it's certainly always beneath the surface, the lack of will, the urge to retreat, to fold up, go to the burrow. At some level, I'm that speechless "egg," hiding in plain sight.

WHAT *Nina* HOPES YOU WILL LEARN FROM HER STORY

"Doing unrectifiable, stupid things is universal and shouldn't stop one from moving forward in life."

SHADOWS

Victoria Zackheim

⋮

There are memories that hover on the periphery of our brains—recollections from childhood, adolescence, and adulthood—threatening to surge forward and wreak havoc on our emotions. Despite our efforts to banish them, they often cling to us with tentacles that cannot be pried away, not even with the passage of time. When we examine the most painful of these memories, we find that they are often stained with remorse or shame.

So what is shame, this ostracism that taunts us like a heckler at a political rally and causes us to withdraw from social interaction, perhaps even from ourselves? I sometimes wonder if shame is the ultimate human drama, a kind of inner theater offering neither intermissions nor emergency exits. It can arrive from an exterior force, making us feel debased and defenseless, or emanate from within, when we know we have done something unethical, illegal, or mean-spirited. I have experienced firsthand the shame resulting from someone's cruelty, at a time when I was too young to understand why I had become the target. I knew only that I was being attacked, and there was nowhere to hide.

When I was a child in the South-Central Los Angeles city of Compton, there were more than a few people who turned their anger against my family for our politics, for my father's role as an educator in the African American community, and for our being Jews. Whether the comments came from classmates, their parents, or my third grade teacher who arrived on our doorstep one afternoon to inform us that we were going to hell unless we converted to Christianity, I felt isolated, an outsider. I also remember feeling shame, and it ran hard and fast, like little racing slot cars shooting along the pathways of my psyche. The most vivid incident occurred in the fifth grade when my teacher, Lucille Van Antwerp, caught me receiving a note from another student. I remember nothing about that note, but I clearly recall how I feared this teacher and was always on guard. She called me to the front of the class and accused me of being arrogant because my father was a school principal. She sneered as she referred to his teaching *on the other side of town*, where most of his students were black. I began to cry. She suddenly laughed and told the children to laugh at me, which they did. Blindsided by this cruelty, I announced through my sobs that my father would have her fired. She laughed again and told the students not to play with me on the playground. If I approached them, they were to point at me, call me a crybaby, and turn their backs on me. One little note, one nasty woman, a few willing children, and my confidence and spirit were shattered for years. Of all the shaming incidents I experienced at the hands of others, I consider this the most shame-filled day of my life. More than a half-century later, I still feel anger and sadness that one woman was able to wield such power over a child.

While this teacher brought me to my knees in shame, I have to admit to an incident of my own doing, from which I created my own shame. Having never revealed this to others, I find myself struggling to form the words.

In the 1970s, I was married and the mother of two. We lived in the foothills of Silicon Valley, where little roads led up to cloistered enclaves of homes with pools and tennis courts. One night, while we were driving along one of those dark roads lit only by the moon, our children nestled in the back seat, a dog ran under the wheels of our car. We felt the thump. I turned and could make out its body writhing.

I felt sick. Even worse, conflicted. I wanted to jump from the car and rush to this poor animal's aid, yet I was unable to move. "Keep driving," I urged quietly, surprised at my own words. My husband wanted to stop, but I was insistent. "It was a bump that we hit," I told the children, and they believed me.

For several days I was withdrawn and pensive, having no idea why I had reacted in a manner that felt inhumane. My husband and I spoke not one word about what had happened. Perhaps his silence mirrored his confusion about why I had urged him to drive away, while mine was based in shame. For weeks, whether I was driving the children to soccer or reading a book, my mind shifted back to that moment. Why had I insisted we leave? I had no answer, yet I was beset by shame.

I accepted the invitation to this anthology because I needed to write about leaving that poor dog, and perhaps to understand how I could have made such a bad decision. As I wrote the first draft, describing the scene, that old sadness and shame rose up yet again. And then, suddenly, I remembered Shadow.

When I was six, my father brought home a black Cocker Spaniel puppy that we named Shadow. He was a playful, cuddly, trusting puppy who romped around our tiny house, piddling on furniture and under the dining room table until my father insisted we put into action all we knew about paper training. We also discovered a wonderful invention: the doggy door. Once Shadow figured out how to jump through the little door, our fenced backyard became his Wonderland for all things exploratory and urinary. Sometimes I would crawl through that door after him, pretending I was a puppy going out for a romp.

I adored Shadow and found great joy in rolling around with him, shrieking both in delight and fear whenever he nipped at my feet. I clearly recall the joys of playing fetch with him, and I can evoke—even six decades later—his sweet puppy smell, how his tongue felt against my cheek, and the silkiness of his fur.

When Shadow was trained enough to play in the unfenced front yard, we would tear through the living room and outside onto the lawn. There were flower beds to avoid and rose bushes to circumvent, neither of which a rambunctious child and her puppy could do. You would have thought we had chosen these plantings as our targets, since we nearly always flattened or deflowered something.

In those days, we didn't worry about strangers pulling children into cars or drug deals going down in our presence. Teenagers didn't carry guns, and gangs were formed more for sports than for mayhem. And while this was a working class city with its share of troubles, I still enjoyed the freedom of playing in my front yard and walking to school with my friends. What fear I experienced came from a house nearby. There were several children living there, two of them quite friendly, but the youngest was, well, strange. He swaggered, though he was only nine or ten, and there was more than just a cockiness about him. Whenever he appeared on the street, I instinctively went into the house and closed the front door—firmly. He had a mean streak to go with that swagger.

One day, Shadow and I were playing in the front yard. As we rolled around on the lawn, I caught a glimpse of the neighbor boy watching us. I was hardly aware of the car moving down our street. Before I could urge the dog inside, the boy called out my dog's name. Innocent and trusting, and always ready to be scratched and petted, Shadow leapt away from me and into the street. Before I could react, I heard the thump followed by the scream. Did you know that dogs actually scream in pain? I turned in time to see Shadow flopping around, blood running from his mouth, and the driver of the car rushing over to him. The dog's screams faded to whimpers, and then he died. The boy, still standing nearby, looked . . . satisfied . . . and walked away. I wept; the driver wept. My father rushed from the house, saw that Shadow was dead, and ran back inside for a blanket. When he returned, I could see that he was weeping, too.

The trauma of watching an animal in the throes of death was so great that I shoved the memory deep into my brain, in a place where it remained for decades. Writing this essay has caused the images of that day to surge forward with a clarity I would rather avoid. However, remembering Shadow's death is, in a strange way, a gift, because it has helped me to identify the link between Shadow and the dog we left behind on the road, and to understand why I urged my husband to drive on. Buried in my memory was the horror of watching my dog die, and years later fragments of that memory made me fearful that my children might be subjected to a similar trauma.

Does this mean I can absolve myself for insisting we abandon a suffering animal, or that I can somehow unlive my mistake, no matter how much regret is wrapped around it? No, but perhaps I can now remove it from the category of *cruelty* more aptly applied to such acts as intentionally calling an animal to its death. Understanding this does not erase my sense of shame, but it softens it, lightens the weightiness of dishonor.

Bad things happen, real things, and children learn from them. I'm not suggesting that my children's lives were diminished because they were spared the sight of a bleeding, suffering animal. What I am saying is that, had we stopped—which we most certainly should have—my children would have learned about compassion and caring for animals. As it happens, they are adults now, with children of their own, and all of them love animals. Love them, respect them, and would never drive away if one were harmed.

As I write, I feel old emotions rising and threatening to renew their grip on me, and I think *Not again!* They will subside, but they will never go away. Shame . . . is shame. Even if we confront it and try to understand why and how it holds us hostage, it can seem as though we are destined to remained victimized by it. Whether it's the shame caused by someone else or the shame we bring upon ourselves, there must be some way to protect our hearts from the kind of emotional storm that can roil for decades, as if our misdeeds are imprinted on a loop that will play interminably.

I tell my students that when we find the courage to write our most painful truths, we are sometimes freed from their grasp. Perhaps speaking this truth will release me. Perhaps I can now place these memories in a box, wrapped in silk, to be carried under my arm. They will always be there as my reminder, but they will no longer be the hazard I cannot escape.

WHAT *Victoria* HOPES READERS WILL TAKE AWAY FROM HER STORY

"It's never too late to open our hearts and release pain and sadness from the past."

PLAYING DEAD UNDER THE FAMILY TREE
Monica Holloway

⋮

My husband cheated on me. I'm just going to say it up front because it's so cliché and stupid-sounding. And while I'm at it, I might as well say that it broke my heart. Seventeen years of marriage, and every night I waited (like an imbecile) to hear the sound of our garage door opening, which meant that Michael was finally home and our evening of chatting about the economy and enjoying a roasted chicken together was finally here.

What I didn't know was that he'd stopped somewhere between work and us.

Getting it off my chest, by the way, didn't bring relief. Also a cliché. Hitting him upside the head with one of his three Emmys didn't help that much either, and although my point was well taken, it made me feel horrible and way worse. It broke his glasses at the right temple. He's legally blind without his progressive lenses, so when I told him what I knew, with tears pouring down my face, he couldn't even see me. So that sucked. When he finally managed to blurt out, "My Emmy's broken!" I told him there were bound to be losses.

There's nowhere to go with that whole "he cheated on me" thing but down, and that's pretty much where I went. Lexipro, an antidepressant, helped a little when paired with a side of Abilify. Still, it did little to quiet my shattering heart.

There were too many moments, hundreds: Michael beaming, his hands involuntarily clutching his chest as I practically skipped down the aisle in my wedding gown, a proud and giddy Michael sashaying around the delivery room with our newborn son in his arms, Michael standing apologetic at the bedroom door, gently knocking as I cried about some unimportant argument we'd had; long rides together through the snowy Southern California mountains; making homemade chili on Academy Awards night; Michael telling me he loved me every single time we'd take off in an airplane. Millions of moments.

Michael was the person who'd nestled into the hospital bed next to me as we watched the faint blinking of our second baby's heart on the ultrasound, having already learned that she wasn't going to make it. Twelve weeks pregnant and so in love with this blinking, this heart we would never know, this baby due on Thanksgiving day. I concentrated on Michael's clear blue eyes through terrible cramping and, when all hell broke loose and the bleeding began, he sobbed with me as we let her go—his cheek against mine so that his tears were my tears, and mine were his.

The history of us, the truth that we really had been in love and that he'd been the only person for me, had to be grieved and sifted through. I could not imagine my life without him. But here I was, alone.

So what really helped? I quit pretending. Another cliché. I woke up— an even worse one. And that's where the clichés stopped and my life began. Not exactly a carefree life, but the one in which I stopped trying to justify my existence by how great my marriage was or by who loved me and who didn't.

Aside from the obvious cataclysmic shift that comes with a kick-to-the-face revelation, there was the matter of shame. Not his shame, although there was plenty of that, too, but *mine*.

This was perplexing to me because I hadn't gone outside the marriage for anything more depraved than enjoying sushi with friends. (Michael didn't like Japanese food.) What did I have to be ashamed of?

Aside from the obvious reasons—I'd been duped, lied to, humiliated— there were feelings about finding myself suddenly alone—in midlife. Who, I wondered, would date *me*—with my light brown mustache and thickening waistline? Had he actually pulled this shit when my ass had flattened out like a hot cow patty, slowly cooling midthigh?

I didn't even *want* to date; I wanted my husband. From the first time I saw him—walking into a party in West Hollywood eighteen years ago— until three minutes before all hell had broken loose in our family room, I'd *always* wanted him. This realization took my hysteria to a whole new level.

Until I could curb the panic and unbearable grief that was threatening to strangle me, Michael would need to physically leave the house. Otherwise, he might end up like his computer—the one that held the love letter that wasn't written to me—the one that now rested at the bottom of our pool. I was completely unglued.

On the Sunday afternoon I confronted him about his affair, and while he was busy collecting his belongings from where I'd tossed them (out onto the street) and scraping his homemade Father's Day cake off his windshield (where I'd smeared it) so he could drive to the Sheraton and away from me, I flopped onto the couch, took a deep breath, and joined Ancestry.com.

Michael represented one-third of my entire family. There was him, our son, Wills, and my sister who, due to circumstances only a psychologist could unravel, was the only person I saw from my family of origin.

So as Michael's taillights rounded the corner of our (now-ironic) white picket fence, my family dropped by almost half. Two family members seemed slim, even to me, who was used to slim.

I'd justified my existence by who was around me. I had a husband and a child. I existed.

I now needed to find something that was mine—something untouched by Michael. If I could determine where I'd come from (or rather from whom), I might understand where I was going.

Holding a wet tissue under my snot-encrusted nose with one hand and typing in my soon-to-be-canceled credit card number with the other, I secured my Ancestry.com online membership. I might have been perimenopausal, and suddenly single-while-bloated, but I was also going to be related—to someone.

After giving up my personal information, the next thing I needed to do was name my family tree—such a weighty decision—to give words to something that encompassed all of my history. I looked at what other people had named their lineage: "Willowkitty's Weedpatch," and "Lot of Tuckers." These offered little inspiration, but I supposed that for most people, a family tree was only an extension of life, not a *whole* life. For me, the existence of family was iffy, so I needed ancestors if I was going to exist.

Perched on the end of the couch with my computer balanced on my knees, I felt alone and way younger than my forty-six years.

Fingers poised over the keys, I visualized the one relative I'd loved with all of my heart and soul: my Granda. And then I remembered one of the last things she said to me in a demented panic as she lingered in the final stages of Alzheimer's: "Where are my people?"

I was afraid of her disappointing gaze if I'd admitted that I was, in fact, her people. In the cyclone of her illness, she had forgotten her love for me, the butter and sugar sandwiches she'd made the two of us on hot summer days, and our Saturday afternoon trips to Miller's Drive-In for root beer floats. I felt that I'd let her down by becoming unrecognizable, unable to make her see that I was—and always would be—hers.

I typed her words carefully, comforted that they were Granda's, distant though she may have been at the time. They'd unknowingly served as a harbinger of what was to come. How could I have known, while sitting next to her nubby, brown upholstered recliner, that there would be a time when I, too, would wonder where everyone went?

The blank box marked "Name Your Family Tree," was now filled in: "Where Are My People?"—a question that I would both answer and ask, many times over.

❖

Suddenly, I couldn't concentrate at all. The absurd reality that my Teflon marriage was dead, hideous, and in a million bloody pieces, smothered me with anguish. My biggest fear, that something would happen to Michael, had become reality. He was gone. I couldn't go to the drugstore for a marriage-fixer-upper or have a trustworthy version of Michael delivered instead of a meatball pizza (our favorite).

I began contemplating how many antidepressants it would take to sleep my way peacefully into death. I couldn't imagine life without him. And then I thought about what a complete asshole he was, and how I wasn't going to kill myself over a jerk like him. I was battling two images of my husband: the stranger who'd betrayed me (clearly an alien wearing a "Michael" suit) and my darling partner who'd been so unbelievably kind to me (even when I had diarrhea).

Absurdly, I was sure that Michael would look different to me now that I knew this awful truth, but he had the same turned-up nose and long fingers, the same small overbite that I'd begged him not to fix. The truth wasn't scribbled across his face as obvious as a cue card written with a black Sharpie. Again, I contemplated taking pills.

But that was fleeting. I had my son, who was going to be shaken to his core already. I would never, in a million years, leave him. In the moment, however, the pain felt that unbearable.

Later, like the cavalry galloping over Bunker Hill, fury reared its powerful and all-consuming head. Now *there* was an emotion that pushed me to action, motivating me out of gloom and despair. Rage felt much more doable than devastation. I fantasized about breaking my husband's kneecaps and pulling the last remaining tufts of hair from his head. I imagined him sorry and living in a brown cardboard box behind Target. That allowed me to stop crying for a few minutes.

I inhaled, trying to quell a full-blown panic attack, as I refocused my attention onto Ancestry.com. Skeptical that any of it would help, I typed my own name into the blank family tree. Immediately, my hands stopped shaking, and I realized that when I typed, my body settled down.

So I typed.

I entered the names I knew: my mom, dad, and grandparent's names —and as I did, Ancestry.com (as if by magic) uncovered new clues— indicated by a tiny leaf unfurling out of the upper right-hand corner of that individual's box.

With new fervor, I clicked on the leaves, sure that I was related to ruddy-faced pioneer women who'd been through way worse than losing the loves of their lives to online porn. Feminists, whose blood I carried in my veins, who'd survived illness, hunger, and all manner of catastrophe. These warriors would give me the hope and strength to suck it up and move on with my horribly broken life.

✺

My first night as a single mother was not spent pacing— nauseous and shaky—but rather gathering my forefathers and foremothers around me. The fuller my tree, the less alone I felt. My first session on Ancestry.com lasted six-and-a-half hours.

✺

I awoke the next morning at 5:00 AM to the sound of Michael walking through the back door. "I want to make Will's breakfast," he said gingerly.

I'd fallen asleep on the couch—Ancestry.com still poised on the screen.

Looking at Michael, I wondered through the fog of waking why he had to announce what he was doing. And then, like acid pouring from the ceiling, tons of metaphorical marital debris began raining down. In that moment, no number of dead ancestors could console me. The truth was, I knew everything, and there was no way to unknow it. Michael had come to tell Wills that he had moved out.

"Wait until he gets home from school tonight," I said, shutting down my computer.

"Maybe I should," he said, looking at me hopefully.

"We can't tell him before school," I repeated, getting up to put my computer away. The nausea I'd escaped the night before suddenly hit, and I raced to shut the bathroom door behind me as I began to unravel.

I turned on the shower to cover my wracking sobs, and slumped down onto the gray and white rug that Michael and I had bought at Bed Bath & Beyond.

As I looked at the tub, the running water, the mirror, it was as if everything was behind Plexiglas. I'd been married to someone I did not know. It had happened to me.

If Michael had been killed, it wouldn't have felt any different.

✴

I yanked off my wedding ring and threw it in the drawer that held deodorant, fingernail clippers, and my secret mustache trimmer. Looking in that drawer, I realized that the solitaire was the least useful thing in there. I slammed it shut, and flopped back down onto the rug.

Michael's footsteps came down the hallway, stopping at the bathroom door. I sat up; indentations of the rug's weave etched on my cheek, and tried to stifle my sobs. He listened for a minute, figured I was in the shower, and walked away. I cried harder.

I wanted him to come in, to tell me I had it all wrong, and at the same time, I wanted him gone. But mostly I wanted him home. Home.

Shock and panic flooded in as I lay on my back, staring at the ceiling: I probably should date. I wanted to vomit. I felt confident and a little relieved. Why *not* take a lot of painkillers? I hated that psycho. I needed to exercise my soon-to-be super-thin body. Michael had an overly large head. I should call friends. I missed Michael's big head. Fuck him.

I got off the rug and blew my nose on toilet paper. Glancing at my blotchy red face, I realized something miraculous: I had 428 new ancestors.

And they weren't just anybody's, they were mine. Those Holloways and Andersons and Matneys existed—I saw their actual signatures on census forms and draft cards—saw black-and-white photographs of great aunts and great, great grandparents with round, wire glasses and white, starched shirts.

Their existence didn't erase how destroyed I was—or the dull dread of facing tomorrow and the day after that. But the *fact* of their existence wove a series of tender, young roots under my beaten, shattered idea of family.

I was heartened, as I gathered my courage to move forward. In the days and months to come, I would need to be sympathetic and kind to my shattered heart, crushed self-esteem, and mangled body image. There was no shame in making bad decisions, only in being defeated by the ones I had already made—unknowingly or otherwise.

It looked impossible from that bathroom rug, and maybe it was, but I was going to have to face all of it, one ancestor at a time.

It was, at the very least, a beginning.

There was no room that day (or for many days after) to look at my own failures or the ways *I'd* let the marriage down. It was not my fault that Michael betrayed me—of that I am sure. But I was surprised and miserable to learn that my need to control everything, giving Michael no leeway to have his feelings (he was my shining knight or he was history), choosing to be a victim my entire life instead of an equal participant in the marriage, had kept me in a denial so complete that only the shattering of my life was strong enough to break it.

What I've learned—and how I'm changing still—is the gift I was given the day my life crumbled. I am enormously grateful for every day. I've worked out my rage, not just about my husband, but about my painful childhood as well, which I thought would be impossible in this lifetime.

I am free—shitty days, tear-stained shirts, hormonal peaks and valleys included—I am able to make *choices,* and not to be blown wherever my imbalances or past insecurities might whisk me.

I learned to love Michael again, the person who'd loved me for most of my adult life, and the one who'd let me down so completely. Forgiveness was not something I'd ever done well.

Here's what I know right now; I *can* live alone. I am safe. I am sorry for so many things. I am broken and whole at the same time. I cannot control everything (or even most things). I love my crazy, uneven, surprising life.

For better or worse, I am wide awake.

WHAT *Monica* HOPES READERS WILL TAKE AWAY FROM HER STORY

"I'm hoping to give a reader the sense that they're not alone because in truth, none of us is completely alone. Shame's big power-wielding club is its ability to alienate and make each of us feel that we are the only ones who have ever been cheated on, humiliated, attacked—fill in the blank. When in fact, we are part of this common family called humanity, and there is not one person who has lived without enormous pain *and* the desire to keep that ache hidden deep inside. We learn to hide grief as children, and it is a great injustice. If we could simply admit our deepest insecurities and pain, we'd find that we are not broken or weak or cruel. We are alive. That's all. Love, peace, great self-esteem—that's what we crave. We can have all of that *and* bear the truth about others and ourselves. I read to bear witness, and I write to give testimony. I pray to be truthful, and of service."

THE MEN WHO STAYED TOO LONG
Amy Friedman

⋮

"Life is sentimental. . . . The biggest thing in people's lives is their loves and dreams and visions."—Jim Harrison

People used to look at me as if I was mad—hell, they still do— when I told them that when I was thirty-nine I married a man who was in prison for murder. When I tell them we were married for seven years and I raised his daughters, they squint in disbelief. "What happened? How could you do that?" they'll ask, and I can hear the unspoken question: *Were you crazy?*

The answer is I wasn't crazy, but it's only recently—nearly twelve years since we divorced—that I've come to better understand what led us into each others' arms.

On the surface, my ex-husband and I couldn't have been more different from each other. He was the only son of a family of Scottish ancestry, raised in a tiny Ontario town with three sisters and a hardworking mother. Will's father had died when he was two, but Will was bright and handsome, athletic and promising until he shunned a college scholarship and chose life as a motorcycle gang member and drug dealer. Before he'd turned thirty he was the father of three children. In stark contrast, I'd grown up Jewish in Shaker Heights, Ohio, eldest daughter of two parents who adored each other. I graduated from a Seven Sisters College, earned a master's degree in creative writing, lived for years in New York City and Berkeley, California, and though I had been married once, I had no children. We didn't know it at the time, but Will and I moved to Kingston, Ontario, Canada in the same year—he to serve his penitentiary time for killing a drug dealer, I to work as a newspaper columnist on Canada's oldest daily.

For years I told people our attraction was, simply, the fruit of a heady brew of chemistry and the fact that the whole world—the prison system and everyone else—fought hard to keep us apart. For years, I believed that our enchantment with each other was the stuff of ordinary rebellion—his and mine. And it was, but I didn't understand until recently that that rebellion originated in the one thing we truly had in common. That something was shame.

In 2002, three years after Will and I divorced, I fell in love with Dennis, a wise and lovely man whose presence in my life no one has ever even thought to question. "You're perfect for each other," everyone said, and we married. For nine years we have shared a life in Los Angeles, the city he was living in when we met. Together we moved into a small house, and together we have taught and written books and shared a happy life. We often welcome people to visit us—our kids and siblings and nieces and nephews and a few close friends. But since we have just one bathroom, and our guest room is in fact Dennis's study, after awhile any extra human presence in our house feels too large. No one ever overstayed their welcome until one day in late autumn an old acquaintance of mine asked if he could visit. And he stayed too long.

While our guest was here, Dennis grumbled quietly whenever we could find any time alone together. I felt guilty and responsible, and I felt frozen. Behind our guest's back, I complained bitterly about this plight to anyone who would listen. Everyone had the same advice: "Tell him to leave. He can stay in a hotel. Or he can go home."

They were right, of course. We had all sorts of reasons to toss him. For instance, from the day he arrived, he bragged about his fabulous trip to Venice, Italy with his girlfriend just three weeks earlier and the glorious hotels they stayed in. His rental car wasn't a tinny Kia—it was a softtop convertible Mustang. He'd brought us a lousy eight-ounce bottle of honey as a housegift, and it wasn't even organic, and every morning he drank a whole pot of coffee and never thought even to buy a pound. He cheerfully told me he had never finished reading my book manuscript even as he crowed about the great notes I had given him on several of his movie scripts. The list of reasons to throw him out went on and on, and it was my responsibility. I'm the person who'd said yes when he asked if he could stay; it was definitely my job to tell him to leave.

But I couldn't do it. Instead I literally gritted my teeth and lived for ten long days with a pit growing ever bigger and harder in the pit of my stomach. Every morning I woke up feeling sick. I envied Dennis because he left the house for work before our guest awoke. I work at home, so each day I rose earlier just to have some time to myself. But every morning when he got up, he popped his head into my study and said, "Don't let me bother you, but could you just print some pages for me? And oh yeah, can you tell me how to get to the Hollywood Bowl? Also, I was wondering if you have any good connections for this terrific playwright I know. And the name of a good Santa Monica restaurant I can take the producer to."

He never once picked up a tab in restaurants or filled the fridge, and on Sunday when we were leaving for the farmers' market and I asked if he wanted to go, he told me he didn't like going to markets, but everything I'd been cooking and buying was just fine.

When he did finally leave, I thought I would celebrate, but I felt even sicker about it. I wished I could laugh the way Dennis was laughing when he told the story to friends, always adding the song Groucho Marx sang in Animal Crackers, "Hooray for Captain Spalding, the African Explorer. Did someone call me *schnorrer*?" People howled.

Even our dogs grew cheerful, sprawling across the guest bed, happy life had returned to normal. But I didn't feel normal. Then one morning I awoke with a vivid memory—remnant of a dream—of the summer I'd moved in with another family. It was just after I graduated from high school. My best friend Tim's parents had bought a rambling house on a beautiful, winding road in Truro, Cape Cod, that summer, and a couple of girlfriends and I had gotten waitressing jobs forty-five minutes down the road, in Chatham. But Chatham was all about loud tourists in a greasy restaurant shouting, "Hey, girl, more clams and fries!" and nights of half-drunken sleep on a rickety cot in a cheap motel.

I was planning only a brief visit to the Kelleys, but when I hitchhiked into Truro, all rolling dunes, wide white beaches and crystal clear ponds, I think I must have decided I wasn't going to leave. Just twenty-six miles from Chatham, Truro felt like another universe—with its land that gently sloped downward from the ocean to the bay. I think I must have known when I knocked on the Kelley's door that I was staying, and remembering that, I suddenly understood. I had come not to visit but to become one of their family.

I didn't understand it—or at least couldn't admit it—but I wanted to become a Kelley. Specifically I wanted to be one of Mr. and Mrs. Kelley's children. I didn't want to be the daughter of two people so boisterously in love they often didn't notice us kids. My parents were too pure. They didn't drink or smoke or curse. They were too naïve. Once, not long before graduation, I'd witnessed their shock upon learning that two of their friends were cheating on their spouses. I'd seen that coming from miles away. And there was more to it. I didn't want to be Jewish, the granddaughter of a Polish immigrant who believed money didn't matter. "You don't take it *vit* you," my grandfather always said, and my dad agreed, outspokenly, firmly, passionately, loudly.

The Kelleys were patrician, cool, soft-spoken. Mrs. Kelley had that sexy Scotch-and-cigarette voice, and though she and her husband liked each other—even loved each other—they didn't fawn over each other. Like my dad, Mr. Kelley was a lawyer—he was even mayor of our town. But his worldview didn't seem so black and white as my father's. In the Kelley house, it was understood that people sometimes cheated on their spouses, that smoking marijuana could be fun, that drinking and swearing were just fine sometimes, that making money was a sport, and fun, and that purity was—well, impossible.

When I knocked, Mrs. Kelley welcomed me into their house—at least I'm fairly certain I was welcome. Perhaps that house was simply big enough to easily absorb another body; or maybe she saw me as a welcome change to her own recalcitrant teens; perhaps she just didn't have the heart to turn me away. Whatever her reasons, she helped me find a chambermaid gig in a nearby motel and moved me into Chris's room.

Chris was Tim's older sister, and she seemed fine with the arrangement. Tim's oldest brother, David, spent his time sitting in a window seat reading Heidegger and Kant and probably never even noticed me. Peter and Lauren, the "little kids," liked me, and I liked them better than I liked the little kids back at my house. So I stayed, and I stayed, on into the dog days, all the way to Labor Day when everyone packed up to leave.

From the first week I was there, Tim resented my presence. By week two, he and I were barely speaking. For the more than four years of our close friendship, we'd spent much of our free time together, talking late into the night. We smoked joints and walked around the parks that ringed Shaker. We told each other our troubles. I'd helped him through his breakups and fixed him up with Laura. He mapped out paths for navigating my complicated feelings for John. But moving in with his family was, apparently, more than he could take, and in that sandy, salty, beautiful place, our exquisite friendship withered. Through college we stayed in touch—I even visited him at Dartmouth once or twice. But after that summer nothing was ever the same between us.

That killed me because without being able to articulate or even understand it, I'd always wanted not just to be close to Tim but to be one of those Kelleys, and if our friendship was gone, so was my reason for living in their world. When I lost Tim, I realize now, I tried to get myself adopted into similar families—almost always Protestants (the Catholics felt too much guilt), with a Muslim or two thrown in for color. The older I grew, the more like my parents I became, but I was forever striving to be different from them. Like my dad I became a fanatic reader and writer, but like my Cape Cod friends, I learned to surf, to ski, to farm. (I even moved to a sheep farm.) Like my mom, I grew to love teaching, but I refused to apply for any kind of permanent teaching job. Like both my parents, I grew up to dislike country clubs but only after spending a good part of my twenties and thirties going to parties at clubs and wishing I belonged. To spite my adoring parents, I married the first time knowing we would likely divorce. Thanks to my grandfather, I never got good at saving or organizing money, and that particularly infuriated me because if Jews are known to be good with anything, it's with dough.

❄️

I wish I could say that by the time I was thirty, or even forty, I'd learned to accept who I was, but when I remembered how much I longed to be a Kelley, I understood that when I met Will, I still wanted to be anyone other than who I was. My desire for this cool, Protestant, hockey-playing man who was obsessed with money—earning and saving and gathering it—was not so much a physical, emotional, spiritual, intellectual attraction to him as it was a desire to alter all those parts of myself. Most of all, because my desire to be someone other than myself was still a secret, hidden and irrational, it had extraordinary power.

From the minute Will and I confessed we were drawn to each other, I was unable to imagine being without this man. I hated those who cautioned me. I railed at those who thought me mad. I despised the system, the whole wide world around us. And I adored him. I was sure if I married a man in prison, a quiet man from a secretive household, a man with two beautiful daughters I took into my heart and my home, that no one would notice I was, in truth, an intellectual Jewess with a penchant for brooding and an embarrassing purity about what the world ought to be like.

When shame descends, it leaves no space to absorb anything else, and it was shame, I see all these years later, that powered both Will and me. He wanted to be anything but the man he had become, and with my help he became again the handsome hockey star, the smart boy with all that overflowing potential. I fell in love with his fantasies of who he was, and he fell in love with mine about myself. I would be beautiful and brave, famous, powerful, rich enough to support him, myself, the girls—the whole damn world if I had to. He and I would write books together, and our books would become wild bestsellers. We were the perfect star-crossed lovers—Cleopatra, the Egyptian queen, and Mark Antony, the already-married general. Like them we would have a tenuous political alliance and we, too, would be willing to commit suicide rather than be captured. Or we were Heloise and Abelard, doomed to a tragic end but writers of exquisite love letters. If anything happened to him, I would be Queen Victoria, dressed in black for forty years after the death of her love.

It was only after our guest departed and I pondered that summer with the Kelleys that I came to understand that our marriage fell apart when Will came home because fantasies evaporate in the light of day. With Will in our home, he could see that I was, in truth, Jewish and brooding, an intellectual who is lousy at organizing money. He saw that I am a snob about snobs, that I could be loud and argumentative, that there is nothing soft-spoken about me. He wanted me to dress better—in heels which I never wear; in makeup, like his sisters. He wanted us to be rich and famous, and I could see we never would be because he was not the handsome, promising hockey star. He was a man who would spend the rest of his life on parole, a man who hadn't lived outside for fourteen years and who had become, in those years, angry and fearful. And suddenly all those things we'd both, separately, felt ashamed of were staring each other in the face, every morning and every night.

If I were a different kind of person, I might have said out loud the things that disappointed me about him and the things that disappointed me about myself. But I see now that I'm the kind of person who needs some time to brood over things—like why I sometimes let guests, and other people—overstay their welcome. I figure things out by writing about them, and that sometimes takes me years. It's who I'll always be:

a Jew, a brooder, the granddaughter of Jewish immigrants who weren't particularly good with money.

WHAT *Amy* HOPES READERS WILL TAKE AWAY FROM HER STORY

"What we see on the outside seldom even scratches the surface of an individual's inner truths."

MY MIDNIGHT COWBOY
Liza Lentini

⋮

When I was fourteen, I started dating a local rocker who played drums in a band called Golden Boyz. Mat (note the one *t*) was the first in a run of alternating trysts between good boy and bad boy which would rally far into adulthood. There was the neuroscientist, the renegade journalist, the Joyce scholar, the bar owner, to name a humble few. Aside from yours truly as common denominator, these men had but one other trait in common: they were all really smart.

That was, until I met my Midnight Cowboy.

When our gazes locked across a smoky bar, my friend Suzie tapped my side with her elbow, leaned close and whispered, "Someone's watching you . . ." Indeed he was, with big, sleepy eyes; deep, bottomless blue lagoons. He was superhero-broad in the chest, with a chin chiseled by a Rodin protégé. His hair was full and dark and perpetually windblown to perfection. Susan straightened her back, flicked her hair, and batted her eyelashes, watching him saunter toward our battered booth. "Could you scooch over?" he asked Suzie, grasping the amber neck of his beer bottle, allowing his eyes to float back at me. Suzie scooched over all right, right in between us. No matter. Our Valentino simply curved around her, his sculpted forearm stretching out on the table. Toward me.

"Well, now," he grinned. "Isn't this cozy?" His voice was slow and low, with a slight Southern drawl that made the words *yeah* and *alright* more honey than molasses.

His smile peaked slightly higher on the left side.

His name? Irrelevant. Merely a temporary moniker, a placeholder, bequeathed before he blossomed into walking sex.

I'm tempted to blame witchcraft, or the alignment of the planets, because until that day I thought "spellbound" was just the stuff of legend.

Three hours later, he offered to walk me home.

I remember that night as being on a movie set, the only two in Tribeca. Impossible, I know, as we were both living then on the island of Manhattan, shipwrecked with eight million other nameless, stressed-out castaways. At the time, I was living in the West Village, its weathered brownstones an idyllic backdrop for the romance about to bloom. The summer had barely begun, the evening came late, and we set out on the laziest quest toward the brightest sunset I'd ever seen over the Hudson River. I learned a lot on that walk. He told me straight off that he "wasn't too good at the job thing," but survived off residuals from a well-played cartoon voice he'd done on a lark several years before.

"What do you do with your days?" I asked.

"Basketball, mostly," he told me, after he thought for a minute. "Gotta stay in shape."

Yes, there were red flags. My friend warned me years ago to avoid the three A's: attorneys, agents, and actors. Any of those without a job who played basketball all day, would be more like a red alert. But then, just when I thought I might run for cover, he bemoaned, "There's just no option, you know, for it not to work out . . . don't know what else I'd do with myself . . . except maybe go back to Tennessee, get some horses, and run my own farm." Without warning, my mind flooded with slow motion images of us two, holding hands as we rode bareback through the Smokey Mountains, laughing and beaming in afterglow.

And that's how my friends and I came to call him Midnight Cowboy.

❁

The next morning, I had to do little arm-twisting to take him to breakfast. We sat outside on one of the last cobbled sidewalks, him in sunglasses, his head mostly down, incognito. "Everything okay?" I asked.

"Sure, yeah, of course," he told me.

As lovely as the night before had been, it was a less-than-lovely morning after. It wasn't my imagination; he was resistant to be seen in the daylight, walked briskly down Bleecker, a little in front of me. Over cappuccino, I asked him the getting-to-know-you question I ask every guy I'm interested in: Have you ever been to jail?

"Huh?" was his response.

"Jail," I repeated. "Ever been?"

He placed his wide-mouthed latte mug down on the table, folded his hands, and looked up toward the sky. Silence. He was thinking. I hadn't asked him to decipher the inaudible squeals of the pantropical dolphin, or to name the last ten recipients of the Nobel Prize. Finally, after serious thought, he returned to Earth and told me, "Not sure. . . . I think maybe . . . but I have to ask my sister. I forget things sometimes."

Hmm.

There were two options here. Either he was a player, or he was an imbecile. I already knew he wasn't a hardened criminal since he was friends with some of my friends. For advice, I called my friend Kathy, the smartest girl I know. "Maybe he's a genius!" Kathy declared. *Aha!* A third option. That had to be it. There was evidence throughout history of genius mistaken for idiocy—just ask young Einstein. I would find Midnight Cowboy's genius if it killed me.

"Bring him to my birthday party," Kathy offered. "I'll let you know what I think." Then she said, "Besides, if the sex is great, who really cares, right?"

We joked and laughed and eventually hung up the phone. That's when the panic set in. The sex wasn't just great. It was life-altering. Breathtaking. Earth-shattering. And, admittedly, addictive. But what if he wasn't a genius, and just a simple dolt? How would that change the way I looked at myself? How others looked at me?

Like most people, when I describe a couple who are of uneven intelligence—one smart, one dumb—a tsunami of images come straight to mind. It's a familiar scene. The bimbette, smiling and cute, and her "cutie pie" gentleman bottle-feeding her every wish. She is young and pretty (at least, at first). He is, in this particular scenario, shining and successful. Though the gentleman avoids dinners in public places for fear he'll be spotted with a certifiable twit and embarrassed by her drunken ditzy diatribes, no one really thinks less of him.

You can laugh and sneer and snicker under your breath, but no matter what, you accept it. It happens. That's life. That's just the way it goes sometimes. Smart men sometimes prefer dumb girls.

But I'd never witnessed it in reverse.

"Besides, if the sex is great, who really cares, right?" Indeed. Oh, what a night. Oh, what a night! There would be many more to come.

MC (as we'd come to call him) didn't want to go to Kathy's birthday party, even though by then it was a full six weeks since we'd started dating. It occurred to me as we were getting ready that we rarely went anywhere in public. We didn't need to. But I'd grown rather fond of him, and was ready to share him with my friends.

The night started off rather awkwardly. We opted to walk to Chelsea from my place, where we met, and I noticed MC was running his hands through his hair a little more than usual.

"Is there something you want to talk about?" I asked.

"Yes," he sighed, stopping in the middle of the sidewalk. "I . . . I'm not gonna . . . be able to . . . spend the night," he said, relieved he'd gotten the words out.

"That's fine," I said. I took his hand so that he wouldn't notice I was disappointed.

"I masturbated twice today," he admitted, after a weighty silence.

"Oh," I said. And then, after a mighty pregnant pause, "Why twice?"

I don't know why I asked. I guess he knew he was coming over, and no matter how dumb he was, a little planning could go a long way.

By now we were at Kathy's building. He opened the wrought iron gate in front of her cement stairs and allowed me to pass in front of him.

"'Cause it felt so good the first time, I thought I'd do it again," he said, as Kathy buzzed us in.

Smart girls might call this foreshadowing.

Things weren't going as swimmingly as I'd hoped. There were a lot of people at Kathy's party, but MC was awkward and quiet, his big eyes sad and scared. Kathy worked so hard to get to know him, even mouthing *gorgeous* behind his back after she first shook his hand. Into the evening, I was elated to see that Kathy and MC were off in a corner chatting. But by the time I'd refreshed my drink, the mood had shifted. I glanced over to my Midnight Cowboy, mouth twisting lazily around a succession of words, my friend Kathy's face slowly melting into an ugly ball of confusion, then freezing that way.

Moments later she stumbled toward me, stunned.

"What happened?" I asked.

"I don't know," she whispered in a trauma victim tone. "I was telling him about a documentary I saw at the Quad and . . . then I have no freaking clue what he was telling me about . . . something about ducks . . . or . . . "

I put my hand on her shoulder and offered Kathy—Dr. Kathy, Ph.D— a consoling look. "It's alright," I assured her. "It will be alright."

Clearly Midnight Cowboy was not prepared for the public.

That was fine with me.

Before long, a month had passed, then another. We'd had our ups (sex) and our downs (money).

One sunny Saturday, after discovering that he only had $5.32 in his bank account, MC hatched a plan. "I'll just return this track suit, and I'll have all this money for us to go to the movies." He opened a Western Beef bag to reveal a track suit, without its tags. I pulled up one soiled, stretched-out knee. Not only had he cut the tags off, but it was clearly worn, wrinkled, and stained. I had to see how this would play out. We went to the sports shop, where he purchased this thing a month ago, miraculously made it through the first round of returns to go to the actual register to collect the funds. After waiting in line for about thirty minutes, we made it to the cashier, some poor, skinny kid who had to muster the courage to tell my big boy to his stunning face that he couldn't accept the suit for obvious reasons.

"Can I talk to a manager?" MC asked, nicely.

The chubby manager was not as nice. "Look," he told us, "I can't take this back. It's damaged."

"No . . . " MC started to argue.

The manager quickly flipped the pants inside. "See? Someone's removed the lining." They asked us to leave.

We weren't going to the movies. I was going to buy us a quick lunch and then I'd have to go home and detox from the experience. As we galloped toward Coffee Shop in Union Square, MC mumbled, "I forgot I took out the lining so the pants would be easier to put on. Too bad they noticed." Not wanting to chastise him, and still hoping against hope that this was all the result of his idiot savant, Mensa IQ, I said, "You know that was a pretty punky thing to do, right?" To which, he had no response.

My roommate at the time, a savvy, admitted ex-lothario, had a little intervention one night as I waited an hour, then another for MC to come by one Friday night.

"Liza, I don't like this," he told me. "I don't like this guy . . . I just know you can't trust him."

I'd never been stood up in my entire life.

"Admit it," he told me, "you're using him for sex." Moi? I don't use people. And certainly not for sex! What kind of a woman would I be if that were true? I protested and he lightheartedly gave me a look.

"Think about it," he said, as he shut the door behind him, leaving me alone, swelling with shame. Not two minutes later, MC shows up at my door, sullen and intense, and with a guitar slung over his back.

"I'm going to play you a little song I wrote," he cooed, taking a seat at the front of the living room as if it were open mike night. He became very serious, and the prolonged finger-picking intro, I was certain, was about to lead into something deeply personal, heartfelt, and potentially tear-jerking. The melody had a bittersweet quality, and admittedly I was lost for a moment, but then very quickly jarred when he coolly uttered the words *fuck you*. I looked around, genuinely confused, long enough for him to resume his skillful strumming and mutter *love me*. Is this the song? Noticing the look of confusion (and fury) on my face, he stopped playing. And started over. The same thing happened a second time around. "Did you just tell me to fuck off?" I asked, poised for a fight.

"It's just my song," he said, deadpan. *Fuck You/Love Me* was the name of this sad, sorry tune, mostly about his ex-girlfriend, with a few New York City heartbreaks thrown into the mix. He stopped singing long enough to say, "I'm trying to tell you, Liza . . . I'm doing my best. I've been such a nice guy my whole life and this is my time to make something of myself. No more Mr. Nice Guy. I have to think of my career first."

I knew what he meant, and there was no need for discussion. I'd heard he was running around with an agent behind my back, and I knew, in my heart, it was true. That was that. I was hurt, sure, but for some reason, all I could do was snicker.

"Did you think it was . . . funny?" he asked, appalled.

"No," I said. "Well, yes. A little. In a sort of Dr. Demento-ish way."

He thought about this, decided it was a compliment, nodded his head and said, "Thanks . . . who's Dr. Demento?"

As the seasons changed, so did my understanding of what it would take to keep MC in the style he was accustomed. He would have to, well . . . do nothing different. As far as rules were concerned, he had none. I would have to learn to turn a blind eye and make a hell of a lot more money, and neither could happen fast enough to keep us together. We met one evening in late September, a time when New York City is blossoming into its most exquisite season: fall. As the sun set over Manhattan, we walked silently around the west side promenade, then up toward Christopher Street, and back down Hudson. We stopped to watch two teams of teenage girls bouncing around a soccer ball, their ponytails flapping like horse tails in the warm autumn wind. Each girl had her focus, but also such innocence. It would be years before any of them worried about breaking up with someone over a walk in their favorite neighborhood.

"I have to go," he said, turning toward me.

No one had spoken for a full hour, and words seemed startling. I nodded. He wasn't coming back. There was no point. The jig was up.

He gave me a hug and when he pulled back, looked at me with scared eyes that seemed to say *please don't be angry*. But how on earth could I be angry? We had a good time, didn't we? I smiled a little. And he sauntered off into the sunset.

So many years have passed, and I hear from MC every now and again, though, appropriately, rarely. He's married, happy. And wouldn't you know, quite the success. Seems he found his home where many other midnight cowboys roam: Hollywood. Looks like he got everything he was looking for. And maybe some true love on the side.

I recently heard from Dr. Kathy, too. We laughed about that funny summer, MC, how he got his name, and how I really should thank him at some point for teaching me what I don't want in a man.

"No one thought that was going to last," she confessed.

I supposed I was one of them, even if I didn't admit it.

"A smart guy with a dumb girl is one thing," she went on, "but a smart girl with a dumb guy . . . now that just goes against nature."

WHAT *Liza* HOPES READERS WILL TAKE AWAY FROM HER STORY

"I hope people will realize that shame can be funny, too."

A BEAUTIFUL PORTRAIT
Tracy J. Thomas

⋮

Every photograph contains a single moment in time. A visceral memory I capture. I choose the subject matter, composition, lighting, depth of field, and, most important, when to release the shutter button.

I became a photographer to hold onto the things I found captivating or beautiful. I became a documentary photographer to weave story with words and images. Photography expresses the contents of my soul and reframes my life with the memories I choose.

There are certain memories, frozen moments in time I cannot control through composition, subject matter, or point of focus. I would rather toss these moments in the trash, but they are embedded in my mind like an uncomfortable self-portrait.

At twelve years old, I stood in front of my vanity mirror, an unrecognizable version of myself. The person staring back at me was an ugly, overweight, pimple-faced girl with pieces of sauerkraut clinging to the wet crown of her greasy auburn hair. My drunken father had just dumped a whole jar of the putrid cabbage, along with its smelly liquid, over my head. He chased me through the house, cornered me in the master bathroom, pinned me against the wall, and, without a second thought, flipped the jar over with an eerie, guttural laugh.

That was the first moment I considered taking my own life and it would not be the last.

My father was loved and revered by many. He had a vibrant personality that drew the masses easily into his fold. What those masses failed to see was the monster that hid just beneath his striking façade; that he was a calculating, manipulative sociopath who exacted his terror underneath their radar.

To grow up in a home with an abusive alcoholic who could also be labeled a "sociopath" was the perfect elixir for the petri dish that grew shame. As a child I felt shame for most everything. I carried it quietly. I carried it deeply. I cradled it tightly to my bosom as if it were an infant in need of suckling. I became the ultimate vehicle for its ability to thrive. Shame became my personal, though unwarranted, mantra.

My first clear memory of my father's abuse was at the age of four.

My mother was out for the evening at a meeting, my younger brother asleep in his crib. I was alone with my father in the living room watching a Disney show. Warmed by my cozy pink feet pajamas, I was stretched out on my belly on the plush shag carpet. My father set his drink down on the bar and lay down on the carpet beside me.

The next memory I have is of feeling paralyzed and frightened with a sick feeling inside my belly. My father lay back on the carpet and lifted me onto his bare chest. He began to slide my body slowly back and forth over his genital area, eventually to the point of unmitigated frenzy.

After the "event," I remember crying in my bedroom with a deep pit of sadness. I looked out the window into the darkness and sobbed "Mommy, Mommy." My bedroom door opened slowly and my hopes were crushed when my father stepped inside. Acting as if nothing had occurred, he asked me why I was crying. I couldn't answer him. I just kept sobbing. He told me in a caring voice, "Don't tell your mommy what happened because she will get mad at you and send you away. Daddy loves his little girl."

His ability to instill fear and shame into me, "his little girl," for the sake of control was uncanny. He broke my spirit with a calculated hubris, shattered my self-worth. Once broken, it became a picnic day of self-indulgent ownership of my soul, with endless years of physical, sexual, and emotional abuse. I became a walking shell.

People asked me as an adult why I didn't just tell someone back then. It wasn't that simple. My father was an expert at ruling by fear, and I was terrified to tell. I have also been asked where my mother was when this was going on. My mother was just as much his victim as the rest of us, doing everything in her power to survive. In my dysfunctional family, it was survival of the fittest. All our energies were spent on our own attempts to make it through, with very little left to spare for others. Self-preservation mode was enacted and the blinders went up so as not to implode any more than we already were.

I was angry with my mother for years. I should have been saved by her. It took a lot of processing for me to finally forgive her, to understand that she was doing all she could.

My father is the one who deserved all my anger.

✳

Evil bodes well in the darkness. It thrives in the shadows that guard it and sits waiting for the opportune moment to strike. That monster, the dark side of my father, was trained to hide in the shadows. He was an ex Special Forces Green Beret, an avid hunter, a skilled survivalist, a crack shot with a case full of guns. There were times when he would rise from his sleep, grab a rifle from his gun case, and yell at us to stay in our rooms. He would then roam up and down the hallway in search of the enemy.

My father was a tormented man who drank incessantly to drown the memories and pain of his own past. His well-trained precision and ability to inflict pain on others was often marred by his inability to handle his liquor. There was the time when he was so drunk he rose from his bed to take a piss, turned in the wrong direction, walked into my bedroom, opened the middle drawer of my vanity, and emptied his bladder all over my diary and favorite sketch pad. After that, he walked to the other side of my bed, crawled under the covers, and began to snore.

By the time I was in junior high school, he was drunk 24/7, had been arrested on several DUIs, and was jobless. We had very little money and my mother struggled to keep the roof over our heads. Bill collectors would call, our electricity was turned off a few times, and we scraped change together just to buy food. I watched my mom shatter into unrecognizable pieces.

Loud arguments were a common occurrence every evening after dinner. Yelling and screaming and crying. I would curl up in a fetal position on my bed under a blanket and cup my ears with my hands, trying not to hear. There were threats and cursing and loud bangs. After several hours of strife, my father would come into my room and offer me a bowl of vanilla ice cream. Vanilla ice cream with chocolate sauce became the temporary Band-Aid for my wounded soul. In fact, to this day, that is one of the only fond memories I have of him.

I carried such shame about my family, I rarely invited my friends to our house for fear they would uncover the ugliness inside the walls. I was afraid if it was revealed, it would somehow be seen as my fault and they wouldn't like me.

For years I harbored a deep guilt because I was never strong enough to protect my mother and brother from my father's rampant sickness. I was the responsible one in the family, the gatekeeper to all the dark secrets; the child who kept everything together so the outer surface would never look amiss. But on the inside I felt dirty and ugly and empty and worthless to the point where I felt deeply shameful about my own worth, my very existence.

In high school, something deep inside of me clicked. A faint lightbulb came on. I began to rebel against the abuse. I became street smart, even though we lived in a small country town.

When I would hear his truck brakes screech as he approached the intersection near the house, I would throw my dresser up against the door, push the screen out of my bedroom window, and escape. I would climb the back fence and run through the fields as fast as my legs could take me to my friend Sharon's house. I made up some excuse, and Sharon and I would clamber onto her rooftop where I would sometimes hide for hours. It was there that I felt the safest and could peek over the roofline to spy on my father through our kitchen window. I was finally in control.

The deeper he fell into the grips of his alcoholism, the braver I became. I learned to outmaneuver and outsmart him. I learned to use my steel-eyed stare as a tool to threaten exposure if he dared to touch me again. I discovered a love for academics and tennis and running and made any excuse to stay late after school in order to avoid his presence. My friend's homes became my homes. Their successful, caring parents became my surrogates, unbeknownst to them. I would study their healthy family dynamics and weigh them against the rampant dysfunction of my own. My coaches and teachers became my life changers. They instilled in me a newfound courage. I realized I had significant talents that could some-day take me far away from this disjointed life.

※

Though I survived my childhood, the ugliness still had a direct effect on my adult self. Once I left that little town for college, I felt a freedom I had never before known. I began to allow my inner child to celebrate and have her voice, but the choices I made were self-destructive. I drank incessantly, ingested every drug imaginable, and hurt as many men as I could. I allowed them to come only so close before the relationship would come to a screeching end.

In fact, I did that with most people, man or woman, lover or friend. I did not for a second feel worthy of a loving relationship. I did not feel worthy of love, period. I had no idea what it felt like to be loved at all. I had to control any situation that might put me in a vulnerable position. I had extreme trust issues. The wounds of my soul were locked up tight with chains and razor wire and a couple of big mean frothy-mouthed guard dogs. No one was ever going to hurt me again.

The tendrils of my shame had a tight grip on my heart to the point that I believed I could not live without it. It had its chokehold when I felt my weakest, and it would scream its way to the surface like a Banshee the minute all things appeared good in my life. It morphed and grew and began to invade every crevice of my being. I knew I could not simply run away from my past. I would have to face it no matter how painful the process.

Knowledge is not the equivalent of taking action. Recognition is a great beginning, but I knew life would continue in an endless circular fashion until I was so tired of revisiting all the bullshit I would have to do something about it.

※

Though I had moved forward with life, earned a degree, landed some good jobs, bought a house, got married, had a baby, and did the whole white picket fence thing, my shame had not dissipated. It continued to fester inside that deep, dark cesspool at the center of my being, determined to crawl its way to the surface again.

It surfaced when I learned I was the one who carried the gene that caused the FG Syndrome my son was born with. It raised its ugly head when my marriage failed. It laughed in my face the day I had to pawn my engagement ring in order to put food on the table so my two-year-old son could eat. It snapped "I told you so" when I didn't get a job, or an A in a class, or I received a tough critique for a piece of my art, or developed writers block.

There I sat, once again, on the ledge of "you are not good enough so you might as well end it." I had recurrent visions of a pistol pointed at my temple. It would take just one bullet, one cocking of the hammer, one pull of the trigger, and this nightmare would fade to black. My father had died years before, but in some deeply twisted way, I still allowed him to have power over me from beyond the grave.

Therapy was my saving grace. Revisiting those memories was the most difficult thing I have ever done. It required a deep personal commitment, a gentle and kind therapist, and a deep resolve to move forward even when I found myself falling back or curled in the fetal position on the couch, sobbing. It was the first time I had actually talked about those deep dark secrets. When the memories became exposed to the light, the snapshots emerged, the truth revealed, and the pain began to fade. I learned to love myself, and recognized the fault lay on my father and not me.

※

I am still a glorious work in progress. The memories are never completely gone, and I don't expect they will ever be. The demons still linger in the shadows and peer out at me from around the corner. The difference now is I am well equipped with the tools I need to slay them.

I am following my passion. My son is beautiful, humorous, independent, thriving, and is the joy of my heart. I have been in a relationship for eleven years, and I am committed to making it last. There will always be some measure of shame; that longtime hitchhiker that left a black tattoo on my soul. I recognize its presence and the role it has played in my past, but I refuse to allow it to have any more power over me.

I cast my shame into a giant bonfire and watch it dissipate like smoke and ash into the heavens. What remains is my strength, my courage, and these words. I allow myself to be embraced by positive, loving people who see the beauty inside my soul and who want me to succeed. I no longer have a need to run, no need to hide, no need to curl up in a fetal position to protect myself. I will live my life with open arms, completely vulnerable.

I choose the subject matter, composition, lighting, and when to release the shutter button.

My life has become a beautiful portrait of love in the making.

WHAT *Tracy* HOPES READERS WILL TAKE AWAY FROM HER STORY

"There is beauty inside each one of us despite the difficulties we may face in this life. We can each be more than 'survivors' of difficult circumstance or atrocity. We can make the decision to thrive and move far beyond our personal shame if we are just gentle with self and maintain an open heart to those in our lives who are willing to help."

FROM EXILE TO REDEMPTION
Julie Silver

⋮

This past December, with palms sweating, mouth dry, knees shaking, I took the podium and spoke to seven thousand Reform Jews on behalf of the Religious Action Center in Washington, D.C.

Up until recently, the lesbian, gay, bisexual, transgendered commu-nity was marginalized: We were the stones that the builders rejected. But now we are the chief cornerstones. I am lesbian, I am a Jew, I am a mother, and I am a partner. Every piece of me is deeply affirmed by the Reform Movement. I not only feel protected by the Religious Action Center, I feel embraced by our community because it has made LGBT equality a priority. I also stand upon the shoulders of those rabbis, cantors, and educators who encouraged me to come out so many years ago. If it weren't for these pioneers, I wouldn't be standing here today. And so because the RAC raises its voice, I can raise my family and we can raise our voice in song, in celebration, or in protest.

I walked off the stage in disbelief as President Obama walked on to thunderous applause. Did I just come out to every Jew in North America? I had never really been "in," but to "out" myself so publicly, in front of so many, with thousands watching online, was something new. I had been singing my songs for years in front of these people, but now the guitar was in its case. Here in this convention hall, the shattered pieces of a broken vessel were coming together. And it wasn't the first time I was healed by this community.

Thirty years ago, I made a mistake. It was a big mistake that could have taken me on a very different journey if it weren't for the people who took my hand and taught me how to lead. Before now, I've never spoken about it.

I spent my childhood summers at an all-girls Jewish sleepaway camp in New England. There are few such camps like this in existence. It was a place where *girls could be girls*. This camp is now over seventy years old. Generations of girls have been raised, strengthened, educated, and empowered here.

The women at camp raised me to become the woman that I am today: a singer, a guitar player, a songwriter, an athlete, an artist, a worship leader, a mother, a partner.

At nine years old, my parents sent my older sister Robin and me to camp. It was the first time either of us had been away from our very typical suburban family life. Robin and I were good girls. Our parents raised us to be of service, to achieve, to be independent. This camp amplified their efforts.

They would pick us up at the end of every summer, and from the back seat of our old Mercury station wagon we, my sister and I, would regale them with two months' worth of stories and songs on the ride home. Of course, it wouldn't be long before we would be in tears, missing camp and counting the days until we would return.

That said, my first summer at camp took some getting used to. Without my parents and familiar surroundings, I was a wreck for a solid week. Nine years old and I could barely brush my own hair. I was so self-conscious and panicked that I would wait until all of the girls in my bunk were asleep before I would use the bathroom because I didn't want anyone to hear me pee. On top of that, every morning during that first week, my bunk counselor, Janice, wearing nothing but a T-shirt and underpants, would wake us up by jumping up and down on our beds; her ample breasts bounced up and down, practically hitting the rafters above us in a frenzied rhythm.

"Julie Silver! Wake up!" she yelled at the top of her lungs. I shut my eyes, and buried myself beneath my Charlie Brown blanket.

As if I wasn't self-conscious enough, in those days it was perfectly acceptable for ten of us to shower together in the old shower house.

"Julie Silver! You still have soap in your hair! I can see it from here. I'm coming over there to help you!"

Oh no, I thought, my naked counselor is coming this way. I braced myself, but there was no way to stop her from holding me under the rusty showerhead and squeezing every bit of excess shampoo from my hair as her breasts brushed against my neck.

✳

One morning as we were all leaving the bunk for flag-raising, she stopped me dead in my tracks.

"Julie Silver! You're wearing flowered underpants. I can see them underneath your shorts. Change into white underpants now please!"

Was I supposed to know these things already? And why, oh why, does she keep using my first and last name to yell at me?

※

After a week of hearing my full name bellowed aloud and after begging my parents to *come rescue me from this hell,* I made it to Friday evening, and the first camp Shabbat service of my life was about to begin.

Picture three hundred girls dressed in white, standing shoulder to shoulder, silently lowering the American and Israeli flags.

Three hundred girls singing *Hatikvah,* the Israeli national anthem.

Three hundred girls sitting on benches in the pine grove, holding prayer books with the sun sinking behind the lake.

I looked around for my sister, Robin, and spotted her with her bunkmates a few rows behind me. I felt such relief to see her there. She gave me a smile. We were together. We were okay.

I listened as every single girl at that camp raised her voice in song. I found myself singing along to songs I had never heard before.

I stared to my left at the row of girls swaying and singing next to me and there was my first camp counselor, Janice, making sure everyone was following along in the light blue prayer books. She looked right at me with such love, such connection, smiled, and said: *"Shabbat shalom,* Julie Silver."

And like that, I was home.

My first crush was on three hundred girls.

I started rinsing my own hair out in the shower—and even started using the bathroom when I needed to go.

Here's what I learned at camp:
How to get along,
To write a song,
To share,
Console a friend,
Live in community,
Express myself,
Give the best of myself,
Be a sister.
I learned how to sail,
Shoot an arrow straight,
Paddle a canoe—
Capsize a canoe—
Play jacks,
Fast-pitch a softball,
Shave my legs,
Make ceramic bowls,
Lay up a basketball,
Make people laugh.

And with five of my best friends cheering me on (from outside the bathroom stall), I figured out how to use tampons for the first time.

I became a guitar player at camp. During my earliest summers, I would sit in the grass and gaze longingly at the girls who already played well, singing Bob Dylan, Bread, Loggins and Messina, Debbie Friedman, and James Taylor. Later, I was the one who played while girls stopped by the cove during rest hour to sing with me.

Truth is, my sister Robin played guitar before I ever thought of playing. And she had a beautiful voice. I took lessons until I was good enough to play and sing with her and we still sing together to this very day. If she hadn't taken this road, my life and work would have been very different.

So I was pretty good and held my own, but it was the encouragement of my camp sisters, especially my *own* sister, that convinced me that I was on the right track. I wasn't anywhere near my potential, but I was beginning to feel like a rock star.

Unfortunately, I began to behave like one.

※

Around this time, my rabbi back in Newton, Massachusetts, was propping me up in front of our congregation and encouraging me to songlead at our temple. I was around fourteen when I was hired by the religious school to teach music. The temple paid me twelve-fifty an hour. I was in heaven.

Within months, I was songleading throughout New England almost every weekend. I taught music, led campfire songs, and played until every request had been taken. I became known for rousing, spirit-filled song sessions for hundreds of high school students all over the Northeast. I was making more money and more music than anyone I knew. I was utterly devoted to the art of songleading and knew I would be committed to gathering people in song for the rest of my life.

Camp song sessions were always the high point of the week. I had nothing more than a guitar and a lousy sound system but I stood on tables and led, just like the women who came before me. Sweating like a professional athlete, singing with everything inside me.

The girls sang so loudly, so enthusiastically, and so beautifully that we became a choir. Day in and day out all summer long I worked on preparing set lists, writing songs, eventually writing Jewish songs and sharing them with the camp.

There are few things more intoxicating than having control over a large group of people, to move an audience, to teach a song, and within moments hear it sung back to you.

Looking back, I have to say that being counted on to lift the spirit of an entire camp and to do it well was a heavier burden than I knew how to handle. My overinflated ego was about to burst.

Being a teenager is hard enough. I was a leader before I even knew how to properly follow. I was standing in front of people before I really knew how to sit and listen—to others, and especially to myself. And although I was going through typical teenage questioning and rebellion, I was looking at my life from a dangerously high perch. On top of it, I was struggling with my sexual identity. I was filled with adolescent passion, angst, stupidity, and arrogance. I loved what I was doing but I lacked the knowledge of my own Jewish history and the texts, or the maturity to understand the meaning and importance of what I was building. I loved this camp, but no amount of "summer camp love" was going to stop the events of Wednesday night, August 6, 1982, from happening.

I don't know why we did it.

No one forced us to do it.

But, I was just foolish enough to think it wouldn't matter to anyone.

My best friend Lisa and I spread out a towel and sat down on the wide-open athletic field next to the tennis courts, underneath bright spotlights, and we lit up a joint. We weren't just smoking pot. We were smoking pot under a massive spotlight in an open field.

Within five minutes, we were busted. The joint was still glowing orange when my counselor ripped it out of my hand, screaming "Julie Silver! *What* are you doing? Get back to the bunk right now! You girls are in big trouble!" Lisa and I walked back to the bunk together, stunned, stoned, and silent.

We woke up the next morning under gray skies that threatened rain. Everyone in the bunk got dressed in sadness and silence. They all knew what had happened the night before but no one knew what was coming next. They looked at me with such disappointment.

I had shamed myself—in my home, in front of the people who counted on me most.

Meanwhile, I was so confident (hubris) and convinced (delusional) of my indispensability at that camp that I thought I was going to get a slap on the wrists. After all, I was a rock star song leader. I walked on water. I wrote the songs that made the young girls cry, for God's sake. No one else could possibly give what I gave to that camp. I strummed a chord and the camp stood at attention and broke out in six-part harmony.

I'm not going anywhere, I thought.

I'm above the law.

❋

Lisa and I were called into the director's office and were told that she wanted to see us separately. She was finishing a conversation on the phone when I walked in. She spun around in her chair, hung up the phone, looked right into my eyes, and calmly said, "Julie Silver. You smoked pot at my camp last night. You broke the law and I can't have it. Go back to the bunk, pack your things, and Marcus, the maintenance man, will drive you home. That was your mother on the phone."

That was *my mother* on the phone.

I took the longest and loneliest walk of my life from the director's office back to the bunk, opened the bathroom stall door, fell to my knees, and threw up.

When I finally sat down next to the toilet on the bathroom floor I read the girls' names that had been written on the walls over the years. Some of them were the mothers of my friends who had gone here as girls. *Micki Levine, '67–'71. Faye Steinberg, '73–'78.* I didn't know these women, but suddenly I felt the stinging shame of getting thrown out of this camp that they helped build, this place I called home. Forty years of the women upon whose shoulders I stand, their names etched forever on the wall next to mine, *Julie Silver '76–'82.* And there was my sister Robin's name written in thick, black ink. My eyes filled with tears.

While we were getting our asses handed to us at the main lodge, the counselors had been instructed to bring the entire camp down to the waterfront so that our departure could be quick and painless.

I never said goodbye to my friends. Nobody ever saw this coming.

Like a humiliated and embarrassed Fraulein Maria leaving the Von Trapp children under the cover of night, leaving the family to whom she had brought fun and laughter and singing, I packed my trunk, picked up my guitar, and went home.

Marcus, the maintenance man, drove me home in the camp van as the rain started to fall. I was so deeply ashamed of myself that I could barely speak to him.

On top of it, my mother's parents were visiting so I had the added shame of getting thrown out in front of my grandparents, which, I am certain, made my parents' embarrassment even more profound.

My parents had just surprised me by showing up unannounced at camp a week earlier, on their twentieth wedding anniversary. I wrote them a song that my whole bunk sang to them. It was one of the sweetest moments, and I could see the pride on their faces as they drove away. I never want to know what it feels like to have your kid write a beautiful song for you and then turn around and she gets thrown out of summer camp days later.

They were blindsided. I was sick with shame.

It's one thing to screw up and suffer the consequences quietly in your own personal life. It's quite another to be thrown out of your favorite place on earth, in the most public of ways, and go home to a gossiping, judgmental town where everybody knows you. Half of those girls at camp came from my hometown. This was going to haunt me for the rest of my life.

There is incredible shame in exile, especially if you have a hand in getting yourself thrown out of the place you helped build. This was more than a fall from grace. This was a public flogging. My parents were humiliated in front of their community. My sister was angry and my friends were ashamed of me. And my guitar sat in the corner of the living room, where I feared it would sit forever.

I went straight to my bedroom and fell asleep until the next day, on top of my blankets, still wearing my sneakers.

The next morning the phone woke me up. It was my rabbi, Robert Miller. I later found out that my mother, in her moment of desperation, had called to tell him what had happened.

"Julie, my love, I'm going to the nursing home before Shabbat, and I want you to come with me. Bring your guitar and sing for these people."

He knew I was born to connect people to each other and sing together even before I did, and somewhere deep inside me, I believe I knew I wanted to teach my love affair and my struggle with Torah in song. It came as naturally to me as breathing. But it was Rabbi Miller who took me by the hand, quietly led me back to the thing I was born to do. One visit to sing at a nursing home and the shattered pieces of my broken vessel were coming together.

I have spent twenty-five years on the road as a Jewish musician and only now have begun to realize that I have carried this event with me everywhere I've gone. It has influenced my choices, informed my work, and made me compassionate and sensitive to people who have been exiled from their homes, even if it was their fault. The redemption and healing that followed is something I am blessed to be able to offer to others.

Ten years after this incident, I was working nights as a deejay at WMJX in Boston. The request line always rang incessantly and since we used playlists, I rarely answered the phone. I don't know why I chose to answer the phone at that moment, but I did and it changed my life forever.

"Is this Julie Silver?"

"Yes it is," I answered, "what would you like to hear tonight?"

"This is Debbie Steinberg, the director of your old camp. We'd love for you to be our head songleader this summer. Are you available?"

You bet I was.

WHAT *Julie* HOPES READERS WILL TAKE AWAY FROM HER STORY

"We are compelled to express ourselves . . . our joys, our hopes, our faith, and our fears. The only path to healing is through sharing our stories with one another."

THE JUMP ROPE LINE
Marcia G. Yerman

:

In today's world, I would have been pegged as a child possessing classic anxiety symptoms—with a side order of sensory issues thrown in. I came by it honestly. It was one of many things I got from my mother, along with her wonderfully witty sense of humor, which she deftly used to deflect her insecurities and worries.

I'm not sure where my mother's fears left off and mine began. Everything was mixed up and enmeshed. Trying to separate out the strands of my entangled neurosis since has been a frequent exercise in internal exploration. It usually leads nowhere. I repeatedly come back to the chicken and egg syndrome. Which came first—the anxiety or the otherness? Or are they inextricably intertwined?

It started as early as preschool, when I was sent to an Orthodox Jewish academy. Why is anyone's guess. My family wasn't overtly religious. Perhaps it was a matter of what was available at the time. The curriculum wasn't steeped in any sort of ritual. My clearest memories are of the soothing daily naptimes on blue cots, and the security of my best friend Helaine. Already, I had begun to replicate the model of the symbiotic and codependent relationship that I had with my mother.

One day, without warning, Helaine didn't show up at school. I promptly fell ill. It was a precursor to the somatic symptoms that would serve as hallmarks of future anxiety. When my mother came to pick me up from this stressful situation (as she would do on other occasions in my childhood), there were no questions. If anything, she was thrilled to have me home with her.

When we got back to the house, it was lunchtime. It must have been an American holiday because both my father and brother were there. When it came time for ice cream, I didn't get any. Requesting some in a plaintive Oliver Twist voice, I was informed by my father that girls with stomachaches didn't eat dessert.

The stomachaches would get worse. In a colossally ill-advised move, partly due to educational testing that neglected to take into account psychological or emotional factors, educational administrators determined that I was "smart enough" to begin elementary school at five-and-a-half. Lost in the shuffle was the small matter of a hypersensitive disposition that someone should have noted. As I grew older, reactive physical symptoms would expand to include tingling in my arms, shortness of breath, or a viselike pressure on my chest. The time the room started to swirl around me was the worst extreme.

I started the new elementary school, but it was an abysmal failure. The teacher, Miss Saks, was young and attractive, but unresponsive to a child that clearly wasn't fitting in. All the other kids knew the words to "America the Beautiful," and how to add numbers. My songbook was comprised of Astaire and Rogers, and the complete score Jimmy Cagney had delivered in *Yankee Doodle Dandy*. My fingers helped me get by if the numbers didn't go higher than ten, and the freckle on my third right digit kept me apprised of which hand was which.

The classroom was in an old-fashioned slate gray and wooden building, a drafty space due to the large-paned windows. There was a piano for music time—a much-needed break from lessons. My goal was to get through the day and survive the raucous bus ride home, where the high-pitched screaming and casual bullying would fray my already stretched-to-the-limit nerves.

My parents held firm that I was now in first grade, and that's where I was going to stay. The principal, a woman of kind demeanor whose name would later grace the school, decided that I needed an older, more seasoned instructor. I was transferred to Miss Franklin's class, and the new, red brick building with the auditorium, cafeteria, and gymnasium. No one was hearing me because I wasn't saying anything. I was afraid to articulate, "This isn't right for me." Besides, was anyone really going to listen?

Miss Franklin immediately took a liking to me. This is more than I can say for the three girls whose territory I was entering. Individual desks made up a grouping where I would complete the final quarter, and my admission was resisted with all the energies only little girls can muster. However, Miss Franklin loved everything about me, especially the elaborate French twist hair-dos and unusual outfits that my mother

meticulously put together for me. ("Inappropriate!" my German therapist would inform me.) Needless to say, they were totally out of step
with the simple bobs, braids, and Brownie uniforms of my contempo-
raries. It was clear that the Girl Scouts would never be on my horizon.
That would have forced my mother to socialize with a group of suburban women she had absolutely nothing in common with—thereby
taxing her already elevated angst level. So my isolation was gradually
cemented, as I became her best friend—as she was mine.

If I didn't particularly enjoy classroom time, lunch and recess
were even worse. Playing outdoors meant joining in games that were
uninteresting, or that I wasn't good at. Jump rope called for a "leader,"
and I was consistently picked last (along with one or two other equally
designated souls). It was against this asphalt setting that my status as
an outsider became apparent to me. Not in tangible words. But in the
actions of others who willfully excluded me. Long before becoming
the creative loner who needed no one, I waited dutifully each day to
be reminded that I would be "bringing up the rear." The shame of this
situation would occasionally be ameliorated when the pariahs were
graced with the gift of being chosen as "leader." It was a false and empty
reward. The few others, filled with gratitude, put their tormentors at the
beginning of the jump rope sequence. I, instead, turned the line inside
out and chose those who had gratuitously crowned me "queen for the
day" to be the very last.

I made friends with a girl named Ruby. I noticed her early on because nobody ever made an effort to speak to her, although she seemed perfectly nice. She never got chosen because she never played. She was always off by herself, alone—the way I would be on days when it was all too much for me.

Ruby wasn't a best friend. In fact, we never saw each other outside of school. Rather, she was a kindred spirit. She wasn't in my class, but we frequently met during free time or while waiting for the bus. She consistently wore pastel colored dresses with white Peter Pan collars, and bobby socks. Her mother also gave her unique hairstyles. They were variations on the same format, which consisted of dividing Ruby's hair into sections and then braiding each area separately. The ends would be finished off with tiny bow barrettes that matched the hue of the clothing Ruby was wearing that day. The result was four braids that stood out perpendicular to Ruby's head.

When we spent time together, Ruby would teach me songs that I had never heard before, invariably focusing on a man named Jesus. Her favorite was "Jesus Loves Me This I Know, For the Bible Tells Me So." When I first presented the song to my parents, they were slightly confused about where I had picked it up. It was a long way from the Jewish folk tunes and prayers of the previous year. But as I described Ruby and how we had met when I noticed that she was totally alone because no one acknowledged her, they were quietly positive about the connection. They supported my outreach to an ostracized child—without quite grasping that I was in the same category. My mother, who was too close to being in the same mold and without the capacity for self-awareness, would never have fully intuited the circumstances. My father, who had made it through World War II as a major in China and India, didn't quite grasp where anxiety and panic could leave you. A master at dealing with the "real world," his coping strategy of choice was denial.

By second grade, Ruby had disappeared. When I asked the teachers about her, I was told that she had been sent "down South" to live with her grandparents. It seemed very odd, and I wasn't sure what it meant. But I was already learning that the people who make up the primary players in the beginning phases of your life could do some strange things and make inexplicable decisions.

❋

Soon there would be major changes in my own life that would put me off-balance. It ratcheted up my persistent nervousness, which left me between projecting an air of apartness and uniqueness.

In grade school, I worked to develop emotional contingency mechanisms after drawing a few conclusions: Gym teachers could be callous and sadistic, librarians encouraged those who liked to read, and being five feet eight inches tall by eleven years old was not the norm. Surprisingly, boys often made better friends than girls. However, by the sixth grade, if you asked your best buddy to dance when the music went on, some Emily Post with a teenage sister informed you that sort of behavior was strongly frowned upon.

By the time I had finally figured out how to navigate elementary school, having found comfort in my affinity for the piano and art (two solitary endeavors), it was time to move on to junior high. Now instead of just one group of kids to adjust to, there would be seven different classes with preteens from the whole northern part of my hometown. I braced myself for what was ahead.

In seventh grade I discovered that I could do well in school. I had caught up with all my older peers. The years of sitting at the kitchen table with my mother, trying to understand my homework as my father and sister yelled from the den that I should be doing it on my own, had finally paid off. I received all A's.

I also discovered that, aside from teachers, principals, and guidance counselors, people did not particularly appreciate smart girls. This was especially true if they were extra tall, wore glasses, and had braces. Some of the girls who were brainy made sure that they did other stuff that would mark them as solidly girly. They laughed at boys whose antics weren't particularly funny, and they had a "crush" on someone they hoped to date. Ninth grade brought new epiphanies, like the way people treated girls very differently based on how they looked. Without glasses and braces, I was now told that I should be a model. Girls whispered behind my back about whether or not I was really pretty; boys still resented me for being too tall, too smart, and—eventually— too outspoken.

A shift in cultural attitudes converged with my move to high school. The popular girls were no longer esteemed, and were held only in high regard by their closely knit group. Football players were trumped by guys who played in a band. An MC5 concert was preferable to a prom. There was a loosening of strictures. Ruby would have found her niche— or at least grown into who she needed to be. She would no longer have been defined as colored. She would have become black.

The existing social structure gave way, broke up, and became reformatted under different labels. The continuum reached farther and now included the druggie, the musician, the geek, the quiet boy who hated sports, the artsy one, and the new term for the girls questioning the status quo—the "women's libber." Suddenly, women in the public eye were speaking about the fact that girls who felt different weren't crazy. Who would have thought that a miscreant society-at-large was partly at fault for my inability to fit in and conform to the system? It was getting easier to pass, even if the anxiety remained constant, and despite some very interesting OCD moves that Adrian Monk would have appreciated.

❋

Graduation offered the promise of a whole new identity, without the emotional baggage of previous history (or so I thought). At seventeen, art school—which was so loosely structured that it sometimes felt like a free-for-all—provided liberation, but not without conflict. I was younger than the average students, who were often four to ten years older than I was and had backgrounds that included the military, previous college degrees, and sometimes a few years in prison.

Everybody had a story filled with personal drama that reflected a strong, analogous thread. It was one of experiential alienation—a history of feeling uncomfortably different and having a way of looking at things that other people didn't understand. We all used creativity to navigate, interpret, and make sense of a world in which people didn't get who we were. In the artistic community, there was nothing too outré. There was no longer shame in marching to a different drummer, just the commonality of being uniquely different. Anything short of psychosis could be the order of the day. I met people who dealt with their issues by drinking at ten in the morning, taking drugs, or waking up in a stranger's bed. I just remained anxious.

After four years of being in a setting that supported a strong sense of individuality, transitioning from a fluid environment back to the rigid hierarchies outside of the art cocoon was difficult. It took a lot of time to learn that the pecking order would remain in full play in all arenas—from the art world to the ranks of feminist activism. But traveling through the different stages of life eventually made these superficial social structures less and less important.

In the long run, my experience as an outsider who felt the isolation of being adrift from others, morphed from an albatross to a position of strength. It was what made me able to see things clearly and be so connected to the plight of the underdog. I felt an invisible thread between myself and those who were treated unfairly—the ones who were different and had no one to advocate for them. It's what pushed me to speak up when other people were being quiet. My exterior has toughened up, if just a bit.

As far as my bouts with anxiety . . . I live in New York City, so I have plenty of company. There have been periods when it has been overwhelming—breakups, change, loss, deaths—circumstances and challenges that have seemed insurmountable. When it takes hold, it does so with a vengeance. However, I try to own it, even on days when it gets the better of me. A ride on the subway watching those talking to the air reminds me that I'm solidly on the safe end of the spectrum.

I still suffer from the existential dilemma, perseveration . . . and the propensity to make everything into a major moral issue or a federal case.

Then again, someone's got to do it.

WHAT *Marcia* HOPES READERS WILL TAKE AWAY FROM HER STORY

"I hope that those who have felt touched by the 'outsider syndrome' will recognize that each individual's uniqueness is an asset—and not a liability."

(MOSTLY) NOT ASHAMED
Rachel Kramer Bussel

⋮

I make a living writing about things that most people would find too private, personal, and uncomfortable to reveal. I left law school for a career writing about sex and dating, in erotic fiction and first-person accounts. I've covered everything from my bukkake fantasies to hooking up with a Top Chef contestant to mommy play. I've posed nude and gotten hate mail. Being open about sex has never felt unnatural, but it took me a very long time to come to terms with this fact: I am a hoarder.

Hoarding, for most people, conjures up gruesome images. Mention it and you're likely to hear about the Collyer Brothers, who died trapped by their own stuff. Hoarding isn't something I take lightly, but I've finally learned that it's not something I can walk around feeling wracked by shame about or chained to my apartment, constantly sorting and cleaning and feeling guilty. Take me or leave me, but you can't take me without my stuff.

As I type this, I'm sitting on my bed, which is now deconstructed, just a mattress on the floor. The frame, which I've been meaning to throw out on the one designated day my Brooklyn apartment allows large items of trash, is tilted sideways against the wall in the middle of the room. Scattered around are hundreds of books and dozens of articles of clothing, along with random items like pillows and padded envelopes, an ironing board that used to support the mattress, an overturned chair, papers from the early 2000s, placed in labeled files with names like *taxes* and *travel,* from back when I made an attempt at organization.

The other two rooms of the home I've lived in for twelve years (half of those years alone) are no better, and likely worse. Clothes spill haphazardly out of all my "dressers," a word I put in quotes because they are where the clothes I feel iffy about go to die. I trip over one of the three dust busters I've purchased in vain attempts to quell my asthma, and keys hide behind magazines and discarded computer parts. It would probably take this entire book to tell you about all the stuff I own, and as attached to it as I am, the point isn't really about the minutiae of my belongings, the most beloved of which are the MacBook Pro I'm writing this on and a huge Hello Kitty stuffed animal that lives on my bed and I talk to when I'm sad.

The point is that while most people would find this state of living unbearable, once I started to let go of my fear of being a hoarder, I was able to make my peace with this twisted state of affairs. For a long time, my place was "messy," as in, "Sorry, we can't go back to my place; it's kind of messy." Invariably, since we're all in New York and most of us are living in small apartments, I would get the same response, "I don't mind messy," or my favorite, "You can blindfold me." But neither of those were acceptable. I was sure that the minute a date or friend even set eyes on my home, they'd ditch me for someone more respectable, someone whose home they didn't have to tiptoe through for fear of breaking a limb—or a DVD. I was sure that if I could just look "put together" on the outside—lipstick in place, long hair shining, tights dazzling—I could subvert people's interest in my home.

I've been in several relationships in which I exclusively went to my partner's home, always clean and cozy, almost like a hotel, by comparison. Even if they nominally accepted this way of life, digs about my home would crop up. "She's never let me see her apartment," my ex-boyfriend told his high school friend during a visit, making me feel like I was somehow falling down on my job as girlfriend by keeping him away.

I was sure that if I embraced an identity as a hoarder, that meant I would never take care of the problem. And I'd tried. A decade ago I hired a woman who charged $50 an hour, a big sum for me at the time. I carefully socked away three hours' worth of savings, but when she arrived, she looked around my room (I had a roommate at the time), dismayed. "I'm sorry, but I can't help you. I only deal with clutter. You might want to think about seeing a therapist about this." She left, and I bawled, ashamed that even a professional thought I was beyond hope. I'd seen websites like Disaster Masters with photos of clients' homes and offices where their stuff was piled all the way to the ceiling, and consoled myself that I wasn't that bad, and even if someday I were to become that incorrigible, there was help, for a price.

When an unexpected financial gift came from my grandmother many years later, I took it. I moved out of my apartment for a week, and let a personal organizer come in. I gave her free reign to pretty much throw out whatever she wanted, save for books and old copies of *The Village Voice*, where I used to write a column. I did my best during those nights away (I stayed at my grandmother's apartment) not to nitpick and obsess over what I might be leaving behind by letting someone else have complete control over my stuff. When I arrived home, my apartment was an odd combination of old and new. It didn't look anything like it had when I left; I could see the floors—all of them! My belongings were carefully nestled in their places. Bookshelves had been built up to the ceiling, stackable, labeled crates contained similar items, such as *computer disks* (remember those?) and *sex toys*.

It was wonderful to look at, and to live in . . . for about two weeks. Then my old ways started to creep in. I'd come home from work and toss a jacket here, a bra there. I'd take items out of my purse and not put them away, in part because I wasn't used to having an away place to put them, and in part, I had to grudgingly learn, because I get some satisfaction out of putting things out in the open, be that on the floor or on my couch or bed. I don't want someone else telling me that I'm doing it wrong; it's my life, and my stuff. At first, I was devastated that after spending over $5,000, it had all been for naught. I was so fixated on the loss of, say, my baby blanket, that I couldn't understand why I'd backslid. I hired my organizer again and we'd sit in the middle room of my apartment. She would hand me piles of clothes to sort and I surprised myself by not wanting to automatically keep them all, just because I'd once worn them, or even once wanted them but never actually wore them.

We made incremental progress, but the more it went on, the more I realized it was too big a job. Every time I even thought about inviting her or anyone else into my home, I got stressed in a very unhealthy way, the panic seeming to rise up inside me, looking for, but not finding, an escape. I wound up admitting to my hoarding in an essay at Salon, and before it was posted, I found myself feeling an extreme sense of relief. There, I said it: I'm a hoarder. Once you've admitted what you think is the worst thing about yourself, nobody else can use that word as a weapon to harm you. They can't fling it as an accusation or reduce you to tears. (Wasn't it Eleanor Roosevelt who said no one can make you feel inferior without your consent?) Coming out as a hoarder had unexpected consequences.

☀

People started telling me their hoarding stories, from parents whose literal baggage they'd had to sort through, to friends who'd never confided in anyone else. A reality show approached me about letting them into my home and filming me throwing out my stuff. I was very tempted, and in all likelihood, if my landlord hadn't been required to sign a legal agreement, I would have done it. The reaction amongst friends and advisors, though, was almost unanimous: Don't go on reality TV. "You don't want to be known only for hoarding," they told me. "You can't control the message." Both things were true, but to my mind, if I could get paid and get free organizing help, who cared about the judgment of strangers? Ultimately, I declined, and am glad I did, but that opportunity forced me to confront how "out" I want to be about hoarding, and my answer, at this point in my life, is very.

I don't say that because I'm proud of my hoarding or see it as a lifestyle choice. I want to have kids, sooner rather than later, and once that happens, my habits will have to change. At the same time, I know I will never be a neat freak or a minimalist. I don't consider myself materialistic, but my stuff gives me comfort. It's mine, all mine. When I'm feeling down, I go to my local charity used bookstore, Housing Works, and browse their $3 galley section. I may walk away with five books, but they are worth far more to me than $15. They are a sign that I can embrace something new, an opportunity to learn, an entrée into a new world. Every item I own tells a story, from the cupcake slippers my grandmother sent me that I've never worn to the dress I bought after a particularly bad breakup to my very first computer that I got at age seventeen when I first went to college. I keep it because someday I may want to see what my teenage self was thinking, and even if I never turn it on, having it handy makes me happy.

I'm sure that there are plenty of ways my life and health would improve if I were able to live more simply. I don't dispute that. Over the years, I've become less clingy about each and every item, and have managed to give away some of my beloved books and even clothes. I know that there will always be opportunities to garner more, to open up new spaces, literally and figuratively. But that sense of dread and foreboding when someone even mentions wanting to see my home or wants to talk me to death about why I carry so many bags around? That has vanished. I still like my home to be my fortress, which I keep under lock and key. I started dating someone two months ago, and I highly doubt I'll be letting him enter my lair any time soon. My apartment is something I feel the need to safeguard, to protect against other's judgments, lest I start judging myself all over again. That's the part that I've let slide: the judgment, the self-hatred, the shame.

My apartment looks pretty much like it did before the organizer swept in over two years ago. You'd probably take one look and think I'd been robbed, or that a bomb exploded, or that I was moving. There are layers and piles all over; you can't see the floor. I often trip over the rubble, and am grateful when a week goes by and I haven't lost my keys. I don't love living in chaos every second of the day, but I've come to accept that the alternative, for whatever reason, isn't something I'm ready for right now.

I'm okay with that, and anyone who isn't, can walk away.

WHAT *Rachel* HOPES READERS WILL TAKE AWAY FROM HER STORY

"You can still strive to be the best person you can be while loving who you are right now, and you don't have to accept other people's standards for what's good or smart or healthy. You can make your own, and sometimes when you do, you learn extraordinary things about yourself."

SACRED

Sharon Doubiago

⋮

(*"sacred: secret,"* Robert Duncan)

Late Saturday sundown, we're running up
from the river. Up the chain link fence, around the sixth grade
from which we've just graduated, the first
class from Hollydale School. If she knows
if I tell her, she looks away. She rides her bike down
the echoey corridors out into the sand dunes of the vast playground

or she heads back
up to Garfield, waits for me
at the light. I cover it

with the new sand
of the new kindergarten sandbox
as would my cocker spaniel, Black Prince George.
I know this is not bad, I know
God's temple, though

defiance, too. I leave myself here. I mark my territory. I pray
to Jesus about the police
confiscating it for their lab, matching it
to my birth certificate at Seaside,
to my admittances at L.A. General, to my impeccable attendance
at Trinity Bible, to my daily school records
accumulated since kindergarten
that can never be escaped, McCarthy's men, their
spy glasses on my every move
seeing that it's true, it's Sharon Lura Edens squatted here

Panic. I look over the sandbox sides, over
the banks of the L.A.
Can I throw that far? I've died ever since.
I was just passing through
when suddenly, most weirdly, I,

the most constipated this side of the Cold War
could not hold it.
Encopresis. No choice. Some part of me

the Sacred, feels good about my solutions
to this most natural of all problems.
Another part feels the secret, the shame. That I do this
to the incoming Kindergartners

but clues and evidences I leave
a part of myself here so as not to forget

There is no Los Angeles River there now
it's covered over by Hollydale Park

part of which, holy of holies, is me

*Encopresis: something unavoidable pressing from within to get out, associated
  with the trauma of sexual abuse.*

MOTHER OF THE YEAR
Kristine Van Raden

⋮

Mother of the Year: First award I ever received. Okay, okay, okay . . . the only award I have *ever* received.

I was five years old. Our local recreation department was sponsoring Kid's Day in the city park. I'd seen the fliers all over town, bright and colorful pictures of happy kids doing happy things. My brothers were all about the bicycle parade and free watermelon. It was the picture on the posters of beautiful dolls clutched in the arms of adoring little "mommies" that got my attention. *"Bring your favorite doll and be judged on cleanliness, appearance and beauty."*

I was a "doll" girl. A girlie-girl whose best friends in the world were Betsy Wetsie, Tiny Tears, and Chatty Cathy. While other kids were playing tag and hide and seek, *my babies* and I were in our special fort, decked out in ruffles and patent leather, sipping tea from little china cups and talking about very important things. I was never more content than when I was caring for them.

The flip side of my love and devotion was the devastation I felt when something went wrong. The time I accidentally left them out all night, scattered about in the yard, I nearly died from guilt. There they were, those who trusted and depended on me most, face down in the dirt—their once-starched ruffles, withered from morning dew.

How could I have been so careless? I knew better. No good mother exposes defenseless babies to vicious neighborhood dogs, or boys for that matter, who would do lord-knows-what to them. The shame of my negligence haunted me because even then I understood that caring for them was *no one's responsibility but my own*; nurturing and protecting them . . . that was my *calling*.

So when I pulled my shiny, red wagon brimming with gorgeous dolls into the park's specially marked arena, the competition paled by comparison. Sure, there were other rosy-cheeked beauties, flashing plastic eyelashes, and pretty dresses. But my "girls" sparkled, as did my devotion to them; and that prize *was* mine!

Walking home that day, with my Mother of the Year award clutched to my chest, any lingering shame from past mistakes was replaced with pride and determination. With the winning of that competition, I knew without question that *mother* was the job I was meant to do.

✵

That award, yellowed and worn thin with age—tacky frame and all—has traveled with me for fifty-plus years, and I have always displayed it with pride.

My destiny was fulfilled when, years later, my husband and I decided that I would be a stay-at-home mom. While he would go off to work every day, I immersed myself in the business of being the parent in charge, the role I had been practicing for all my life. My girls were the focus of my infinite love, time, and attention. My sole (soul) purpose was to be the very best mother humanly possible.

As any Mother of the Year surely knows, a significant clause in the job description includes raising children with the end in mind; that being, "letting them go." While we would do *anything* to keep them safe, it is crucial for their own success to let them go. Both of my daughters tested their independence early. Both lived abroad as exchange students while in high school, then again in college. Oh, how I hated giving them up, but was convinced that their lives would be better for the experiences . . . and anyone knows that a good mother denies her own yearnings for the betterment of her child.

When my youngest daughter, Kate, came back from her first yearlong study abroad, I wasn't surprised that while she seemed pleased to be home, she also seemed somewhat distant and uncomfortable. I expected a period of readjustment. She had experienced an independence that couldn't be quelled, a major accomplishment that was hers alone.

Her senior year was not easy. She was bored and restless and had a hard time connecting with the friends she had before her exchange. She kept to herself more and more. We were all anxious for graduation and the freedom that moving on to college represented for her.

She went to an excellent university with awards and scholarships that most parents dream about. She worked hard as we knew she would. Instead of growing more confident with her abilities and newfound independence, she seemed more unsettled—more and more closed off from us, primarily from me. It was hard to get her to come home for visits, return calls or emails. When we did connect, she was vague about her life at school, friends, classes.

✳

I don't know which came first, the modeling or the weight loss.

While managing a full class load, she started working with various photographers and seemingly found instant success. With her success, I watched my daughter morph into a beauty-by-design. The hair became blonder; the nails manicured. The teeth, whitened, and her waistline sculpted by hours and hours in the gym.

I asked questions. I pushed, snooped, and prodded. I worried and then worried some more. Initially I worried more about her losing herself in an industry that seems to chew up young women and spit them out than I did about the weight loss. But over time, the weight loss became compulsive. I speculated that a day did not go by without intense exercise. When she did come home for a brief visit, she refused to eat what I prepared and instead consumed large quantities of fat-free this and that, things she bought for herself.

I tried to get her to talk to me, but she would only say that she was fine. The more I asked, the more closed-off she became. She sensed my desperation and she resented it. It was clear that she didn't want my help, my counsel, my cooking, my *anything*. Where I had once felt such confidence, I only felt overwhelming inadequacy; an utter failure at the one thing that meant the most to me. I couldn't fix what was wrong in her life, no matter how desperately I wanted to.

I will never forget the day she surprised me by showing up at our home. She walked through the living room toward me and said, "Ta-da, size *zero* jeans, my first pair." She was beaming, and so gaunt that I was afraid I might not have recognized her if she passed me on the street.

Her life as an independent adult continued after graduation. She lived with friends, worked diligently supporting herself with her modeling. Her diet and exercise routine became the most important things in her life. She often missed family functions, or time with friends because she needed to exercise.

My sense of helplessness and shame grew as my daughter appeared to be wasting away. There isn't anything more devastating than watching someone you love with your whole heart and soul disappear right before your eyes. All I wanted to do was love her—love her back to herself, love her back to wellness, love her back to me. I couldn't believe I was failing my child, but no doubt about it, I was.

She finally grew so intolerant of my worry that all she could think to do was escape. So she took a job on the other side of the country, where she could fight her battles unencumbered by the guilt and shame she must have felt every time she looked into my eyes. She lived in Manhattan for nearly a year, absorbed into the youthful culture working two to three jobs just to get by. I knew she was exhausted, often submerged in sadness, but I didn't know that she was starving to death, literally.

By some miracle, Kate was able to take a long weekend off work and agreed to come home for those few days. She stepped off the plane looking like she was returning from war. She was more frail than I had ever seen, her eyes punctuated by dark circles and sharp cheek bones. All she wanted to do was sleep; all I wanted to do was end her suffering. When she finally woke up, she scoured the fridge and cupboards for something she could eat. Her time with us was tense and filled with anxiety, both hers and ours.

Three desperate days later, she was scheduled to return to New York and I knew that if I begged her to stay, I might drive her away for good. I couldn't risk unleashing the hysteria that boiled under my fragile surface. In the car ride on the way to the airport she started to cry. I knew the words that she was trying to get out were those I had feared, but also those I had expected.

"Mom, Dad," she said. "I have to tell you something. I've been struggling with food. I think I have an eating disorder. I think I am anorexic."

There it was. The Beast exposed! Finally, something to battle against. I wanted to fight, but I didn't yet understand the enemy. I wanted to scream until no sound was left inside me. How could my child, the one whom I have loved without reservation or limit have an eating disorder? How could my child, to whom I have devoted my life to be racked with self-doubt and life-threatening insecurities? Instead of screaming like a wild animal, I felt an icy numb take over. I could hear myself asking logical questions, offering reasonable solutions. Keeping the terror at bay until I could collect myself, figure out a strategy, and get to work.

Determined and promising to fight this thing harder and better, she kissed her dad and me goodbye. And as I absorbed each step she took away from me, the hysteria I had been suppressing exploded for everyone to see. I was so ashamed that I couldn't even look at my husband. She was *my job, my calling* . . . and I had failed. Her self-degradation had to be my fault. I must have made grave mistakes and she was paying the consequences. I have always known that what goes right in a child's life isn't necessarily credited to the mother, but what goes wrong certainly is.

Unable to manage her own survival, Kate agreed several weeks later to come home and get help. She stepped off the plane once again and we drove her straight to an eating disorder specialist. After the doctor examined Kate, we walked across the street and checked her in to the hospital, where she was taken in a wheelchair to the cardiac unit.

It all felt like someone else's tragic story. Nothing made sense . . . nothing fit. If I could only concentrate enough, I would be able to find order, even a solution, and life could return to normal. Instead, there was chaos: monitors, medication, strangers constantly checking this and probing that. I wanted to do something, but all I could do was watch, and then leave the room when I couldn't contain my agony.

Kate was frightened, agitated, and confused. While she knew she needed help, she looked at me through eyes of accusation, telling me without words that I had betrayed her. She felt trapped and exposed.

Very few understand anything about the condition. People usually assume that it is a disease of vanity. Anorexia can look like a choice; a choice to emulate the surreal bodies that grace the covers of magazines or sell expensive underwear. In truth, anorexia becomes a prison, trapping its inmates in a dark and isolated cell of self-loathing and abuse. Who would choose that?

She begged us not to tell anyone. So many family and friends—people who loved her and treasured her place in their lives—they knew she was home, but inaccessible. For months we hid out, none of us wanting to be exposed or have to explain. Kate didn't want people to know because she didn't want their opinions of her to change. She didn't want to be perceived as mentally ill, and if people knew that she was suffering with anorexia, she would always be *that* person in their minds, a person to be watched, judged, and pitied.

I welcomed the exile. I couldn't face those who expected our family to be what it had always been, knowing that we had become something I couldn't comprehend or explain. On occasion, when I did run into someone I knew, I tried to pretend that everything was okay, but that always ended badly . . . usually resulting with me breaking down into a tsunami of tears, or finding a lump in my throat the size of Mount Everest, rendering me unable to speak at all. Really, all I could manage was the facade of being strong for Kate and then falling completely apart when she wasn't watching. I was never ashamed of Kate's condition, but of my inability to protect her from it.

If you read early literature (and I read it all) about anorexia, *controlling mother* is mentioned as a foundation upon which the condition can develop. So I racked my brain day and night. Was I controlling? Did I love her too much, indulge her . . . spoil her? Did I hold the reins too tight? Restrict her independence? Did I set the bar too high, not high enough? Every minute of every day as I tried to understand the disease and anything that might offer help, I tore myself apart trying to find the cause within me. I was more than willing to take any blame, if by doing so I could help unburden her.

I swear I relived every conversation I ever had with her . . . the one where I said, "You can't wear that; you look kinda slutty." Did that do it? Was that the piece that tipped the scale? Or, "Honey, you can't eat that entire package of Oreos before dinner." "No dessert until you finish your vegetables." "That shirt looks a little small."

In the thick of rearing my daughters all of this seemed like what a mother was supposed to do. First you love them. Then you feed and clothe them. You offer up appropriate consequences; you guide, nurture, correct, and direct. But was I critical, demeaning, shallow? Did I make too big a deal about my own appearance, or a disappointing five-pound weight gain? Did I care too much, or not enough?

So one impossible day after another, we suffered . . . side by side. Each feeling like the shame consuming us might just kill us. I, struggling with the paralyzing pain of accepting my own imperfections and failures, letting go of the one thing that I thought defined me, and my daughter, fighting her way back from an unattainable goal of perfection that had come to define her.

Slowly and with abundant courage, Kate pursued wellness. Doing so meant exposing her reality. It meant confiding in a faithful few, each one accepting her as the remarkable human being she had always been. It meant that when she studied loving faces for any shred of judgment and found none, she could shed a few more bits of the shame she had carried.

On about one hundred occasions, I gave Kate permission to blame me. Somehow it felt that if she could, she might be able to identify a source and therefore a means of fighting her way back. She never did. She refused to punish me, or anyone else. Instead she worked courageously toward her own self-acceptance. And as she did, I started to find my own.

It has been three years of learning that loving someone with all your might still can't keep them safe and spared from heartache and anguish. It has been three years of a journey that has made my family more open, more respectful of one another, and more authentic. It has been three years of looking at and accepting my own shortcomings as a person and as a mother.

❋

I have come so close to demolishing that Mother of the Year award that has come to serve as a constant reminder of my shame, but something always stopped me.

We've recently moved into a new home, and as I unpacked that once treasured piece of my history, I think I finally came to understand its true meaning. Being a devoted mother doesn't mean there will be no pain. It means that when the pain is present, so am I. It means that at the end of the day, at the end of the skirmish or hellacious battle, my best is enough. That just because I care desperately doesn't mean I can change the course of a life—not mine, or anyone else's. Finally, that one of the greatest gifts we can give our children and therefore ourselves is the grace to fall flat and then to get up again and again and again.

Just this past Mother's Day, I actually got a Mother of the Year award from Kate. It looked a little like something you'd earn after your prized rabbit took first place at the county fair. She said she thought it was time that I had a real one, one that really counted. She signed it, "All my love, and I have never doubted that you have given me all of yours."

※

She was right . . . *this one really counted.*

WHAT *Kristine* HOPES READERS WILL TAKE AWAY FROM HER STORY

"Each one of us carries shame that we pray never surfaces, secrets that we work ceaselessly to keep hidden. It is my hope, that by shining a light on my own personal shame, you might know that you are not alone with those dark, miserable feelings . . . and that there is a light at the end of the tunnel if you are willing to begin with just one small step."

I LOVE ME, I LOVE ME NOT
Kate Van Raden

⋮

I plunge a hand beneath the bed and search the dark for my extra blanket. Even in the middle of a New York summer, my fingers and toes ache with the cold. Contracting and releasing all the muscles in my body, I am determined not to get up. I seize the edge of a comforter and wind it tightly around my body. *This is bullshit,* I think, clenching my teeth.

For a moment, I slow my breathing to listen to the empty creaking inside the apartment, the methodical ticking of the wall clock in the kitchen. After a while, I relax back into my pillow, sure that everyone else is sleeping soundly. *One one-thousand, two one-thousand*—I flip maniacally between counting and conjuring any relaxing memory I can. I search the crevasses for something that resembles sleepy, but I know in that moment that I am spending another night in fitful torment.

I can't bear lying here anymore, the flulike feeling invading my muscles and stomach with every breath. I shepherd my feet to the floor and, quaking like a leaf, teeter through the darkness into the gaping black of the kitchen. "Oh god, I just want to sleep," I grumble to myself, pausing for a minute to listen for movement. Then tip-toeing on cold tiles, I cross the room. Crouching in front of the fridge, I stealthily creak the door open, blinking back at the glaring light.

No need to scan the fridge; I know what I am looking for and just where to find it. With my hand on the lid of a jar of peanut butter, I freeze again to make sure no one is coming, then wrench the jar from the door and release the lid. Hot swelling panic overtakes my restraint to pause and retrieve a spoon from the other side of the room. I thrust a finger deep into the jar and up to my mouth. The stuff never touches my tongue long enough to taste it; to feel its weight. That's the rule. Dig, repeat, repeat, repeat; I gulp down blob after blob.

For those first few seconds, my mind surrenders to a feeding frenzy—blank, but riddled with tangible panic. During those moments, I am not a girl watching her weight. Devoid of a tongue that can taste, or a stomach that knows hunger or satiation, a nose that can smell, or ears that can hear. I am just a goal: Get as much of this inside as possible before she comes back.

The refrigerator stalls, snapping me back to the present. Suddenly, as if from sleepwalking, I become aware that I am still perched on my toes, clutching the half-empty jar of peanut butter, grubby little fingers hovering in the air. The horror of the moment consumes me as I bolt to my feet. Drenched in sweat, I rush back into my room, throwing the door closed and cower behind it. I toss the jar under my bed, and dive beneath the covers. "I wonder if they were planning to have that for breakfast?" I ask myself beneath a wave of humiliation. "I'll get up first thing, run to the store, and replace it before anyone gets up."

This was not the first time I'd found myself crouched in the kitchen, eating straight out of the fridge in the middle of the night. I knew the drill. Within moments, the shoveling would slow. Inevitably I would take a breath, and in that moment, she would be there.

Oh my god, are you fucking kidding me? I would call you a disgusting pig, but that's far too kind for you. Don't you have any self-respect? Do you know how many grams of fat you just ate? That was at least a weeks worth of calories for a skinny person, which I know I don't have to remind you, You are not! You are, however, a waste of space—lots and lots of space. And, you're too weak to throw up. That's what a less self-indulgent person would do in this situation. God. Exhale.

Here I am again, I think, now with a different problem. This one, no easier to sleep with: my stomach already beginning to revolt. I roll on my side, allowing my tummy to expand into the open air, unencumbered; to stretch as far as it can. I feel pockets of gas bubbling up in my belly as my digestion tries to rise to the challenge. Within mere minutes the sheet beneath me is soaked through with sweat. I can barely allow myself to consider what condition my body is in to swing so seamlessly between bone-chilling, aching, blue cold . . . and throbbing, sweating, feverishly hot with just a few bites of food. Every surface of my body feeling like fire. I roll over and over, trying to find a cool surface on the bed to press my hot skin against. After an hour or so, my swollen stomach settles and the exhaustion of the experience takes me, finally, into a guilt-ridden, restless sleep until the alarm breaks through and rescues me.

Before my eyes even see the first light of day, my stomach is in my throat. *Fuck, what have I done,* I think. I don't want to open my eyes. I never want to open them again, as tears stream down my cheeks. If only I were stronger, I could give this all up with dignity. But I'm not, I'm disgusting and I'm weak. I can never do the right thing because I'm a coward. I sob silently with my face buried in the pillow.

My thoughts urge me on.

✳

I can't help you if you don't listen to me. Just get up! Dash to the store and get the stuff. Run back here and replace it before anyone gets up. Then get to the gym for a few hours of cardio before work. Then, go for a run on your lunch break, and lift weights before your shift tonight. If you stick with the plan, take the diet pills, and don't go above one protein shake today, I might be able to salvage something worthwhile about you. I'm serious . . . sleep at a stranger's place tonight if you have to, so that you can't eat again . . . that is, if anyone would even have you.

I shudder now, thinking back on those nights. Hours of tossing and turning, fighting the need to eat, willing my body to sleep. I was living in New York City at the time and working three jobs to support my cost of living. Between modeling, full-time office work, and managing a night shift at the local gym, I worked diligently to keep my mind distracted for at least twenty-one hours a day. The cost of going through the motions of living nearly killed me. I had to pretend, eight hours a day, that I was present enough to entertain clients, take important messages, and look somewhat professional. During my night shift at the gym, I actually worked out behind the desk, trying to look like I cared about the members who had paid to come and exercise there. And then there was the modeling. No matter the job, the client, the clothes, the photographer, I had to disguise the dysmorphia that had me convinced I was an enormous embarrassment and pretend to be the svelte, fashionable woman I was being paid to be.

It worked for all of a year, and then I broke. I knew one day while walking to the gym for yet another six-hour workout, belly bulging from the night before, that I wasn't going to survive living like this much longer. It certainly didn't feel courageous at the time, deciding to give up the only thing that I believed I had to show for myself. But, the iron will I had crafted to manage my eating disorder was in shambles and I realized that I wanted to live more than I wanted to control my weight. With no clue of how to proceed, I made what seemed like the only choice I had left: complete surrender.

I conceded to myself and eventually to my family and friends that I could no longer sustain the path I had been on. My single-minded obsession would have to go in favor of learning to live this curse with grace. I knew I could bear any suffering to spare the people that loved me, and if I could honor them with my work, I could tolerate the humiliation of failing.

And so I began. Upon arriving home to Oregon, I was admitted to the hospital. I spent three weeks hooked up to heart monitors and a defibrillating vest at night. There, I was force-fattened; cameras monitored me at all times. Nurses reviewed my tray after every meal to make sure I hadn't hidden anything in empty butter or pudding containers. With no adjustment period, I was eating full-fat and full-sugar foods, things that were totally off limits for years. My urine was measured every day to ensure that I wasn't bingeing on water. Nurses had to accompany me to the toilet and shower to be sure I wasn't vomiting. By the second day, I asked to be sedated for the remainder of my stay, and was obliged.

❋

After three hellish weeks living in the cardiac ward at the local hospital, I entered an eight-hour-a-day treatment program where, on top of the force-fattening, I would have to directly confront my eating disorder. I said the hard words. I told rooms full of people how I believed that indulging in the pleasure of food (or really anything that gave me selfish pleasure) made me disgusting and weak; how I felt that I shouldn't need it, want it, or even have it. I sat in fluorescently lit hospital rooms with other patients and stirred plates of peas with revulsion. I cried; and then I cried more. With the crying, I was able to release every moment of agony that I had endured alone.

In the evenings, collapsed on my parents' couch, my mother, father, and I could sometimes manage a laugh about the ridiculousness of this fucking battle. Other nights, my mother would serve up beautiful, healthy appetizers to please me; low-fat casseroles and colorful salads. But after adding up—hummus: twelve grams of fat, twenty-four carbs; chicken casserole (low-fat cheese, tortillas, olives): thirty-six grams of fat, sixty carbs; salad dressing: fifteen grams of fat, thirty grams of sugar—my chin would give way to a slow quiver that would quietly spread across my face, finally erupting into big, rolling sobs. On these nights, I would feel so much shame. I chastised myself inwardly for being too weak for anorexia and too weak for recovery. Often I was completely overwhelmed with failure and all I could think to do was go to bed. Those nights I prayed that I wouldn't wake up the next morning. Occasionally I could find what it took to agree to start fresh the next day.

My day-treatment program often gave me homework assignments, like: "Go out to dinner (at an actual restaurant with people in it) and eat pasta . . . *in front of everyone.*" I did it. "Reintegrate nuts into your diet." I did it. "Experiment with eating on a date," check! "Go out with your family this weekend and have pizza." (That one has taken a few years.)

The months passed and little by little, I ate. Little by little, I opened up and could speak about my fears and the dreaded voice inside my head that constantly reminded me that I was worthless. I counted the milestones like "Now I can eat on my own, so maybe it's time to try a part-time job." Or "Now I can eat dinner without feeling that I don't deserve it. . . . So perhaps I should experiment with having an apartment that I can stay at sometimes by myself." And then finally "I think I'm ready to live alone, work full-time, and see how it goes." One small step at a time, or learning to forgive myself for the ones I couldn't take, I managed to see light where there had only been total darkness.

There is no logical reason for me, a bright capable person, to believe I will never be good enough. Maybe I could pin some of the blame on society . . . the media, advertising, fashion trends, or cruel classmates. But ever so slowly, the tyrannical voice inside my head became all I could hear. I believed with every fiber of my being that I was a waste of space . . . good for nothing.

In the last year, I have started to feel that I can manage the challenges of a relationship along with the challenges of my anorexia. I have even felt, at times, worthy of a partner. So I began going on dates, practicing self-care skills, as well as new boundaries that would support my recovery. By swallowing my pride (another almost impossible thing to swallow), I was able to open up my life to the gifts that were waiting to come in. I never imagined that this affliction would reward me in any way, but today I am able to be more honest with the people I trust. I am slowly starting to see myself through their eyes.

I count their acceptance of the real me, just the way I am, as one of the greatest blessings of my life. Won with my own blood and tears (but certainly not mine alone), I am closer now to loving the *me* that is. Through several years of learning about eating disorders, my core belief today is that the anatomy of my brain simply developed in such a way that anorexia was, and is, my destiny. There was no turning point for me, no environmental factor that caused me to develop anorexia. A simple flaw in my physical development (and that of thousands of others) makes me susceptible to the rigged thinking that triggers an eating disorder. There is no other explanation for pushing my body beyond a normal limit of suffering, where losing consciousness was barely more than an inconvenience of daily life. I believe that I pushed myself to a state of being physically numb, where the only pain was mental. Then I could abuse my body in any way, to help manage the mental and emotional challenges of life.

❊

Today, I go to the gym for a reasonable workout. I am not anxious about going, and I am not afraid of how I will look to those around me. It doesn't take me two hours to get dressed anymore. While I still compare myself with every person on the street or the bus, looking for shreds of evidence that I am as good as she is, I am no longer paralyzed by the belief that everyone is judging me just as harshly. Through the process of emotionally traumatizing several young men (you know who you are, and I'm eternally grateful), I have even regained some appreciation for my femininity and, dare I say (gasp), body.

There was no path around this one, just the ugly, shameful, honest path right through the middle of it. I can now say that after waging war with myself, my thoughts, my beliefs for the past five years, I try to be proud of who I am instead of how I look. That is not always easy for me, as I know it isn't for most people. But, I am no longer putting life on hold, waiting to be a size zero. I can enjoy all the wonderful things that this body can do . . . and I say that . . . shamelessly.

WHAT *Kate* HOPES READERS WILL TAKE AWAY FROM HER STORY

"I hope that through reading my words, some other human being will be able to open their heart, share the darkness inside them that they believe makes them 'bad,' and strip that darkness of the power it has been allowed to have on that life."

RAISING A COWBIRD
Jenny Rough

⋮

One afternoon last July, Ron and I were sitting on our deck watching wild turkey scratch into a pile of pine needles looking for bugs. One minute, we were eating Havarti on crackers and sipping wine, and the next minute, I was crying. It was Saturday. We were three hours into our summer vacation in Colorado, and we were finally coming to terms with the fact that we weren't going to have a baby.

We had been trying for six years. I had miscarried one child, and never conceived again. With a debilitating case of endometriosis, I was debating a hysterectomy. My consultation with a surgeon—an appointment I kept canceling and rescheduling—was set for the Wednesday after vacation. Buckling to my knees. Staggering into public bathrooms and crouching on grime-soaked floors. Hemorrhaging through a tampon and backup pad. Choking back sobs and clutching my stomach underneath a conference table at the editorial offices of a magazine. I was ready for it to end. The bleeding. The cramping. The pain. Those awful moments. But I kept putting off the operation because I wasn't ready for the other ending. Motherhood.

While I'd known for a long time that I was never going to be the kind of woman who popped out a big brood and set aside my career to stay at home and raise kids, I always believed Ron and I would have at least one child. A small family. The three of us. I felt the certainty of it deep in my bones. So I gritted my teeth and endured the pain of endometriosis each month as I waited for our second miraculous conception. The baby I was sure I'd carry to full-term. Our son or daughter.

In my mind, having one child felt manageable. I wanted to continue my work as a freelance magazine writer. I loved my job, but my income was sporadic and unimpressive. And that afternoon on the deck in Colorado, it hit me: I wasn't giving my husband offspring or steady income. All the other wives I knew added one or the other to the marriage, if not both. My parents used to have a food bowl for their cat that read *Useless* along the side. That's how I felt. Useless.

"What if you showed up at your company and worked a full month, and then the next, and then the next, and you were still waiting for a paycheck to arrive in the mailbox?" I asked Ron. I could make a similar argument for trying to conceive. Month after month I tracked my cycle, ate a fertility-friendly diet, and had plenty of sex. But when I checked my womb, it was empty.

"Well, I'd quit," Ron said.

And so I agonized for hours. Should I abandon a writing career, even though I loved it? And should I give up on parenthood—go ahead with the surgery—even though it meant Ron and I would never have a child?

I cried so hard that night, my left eye was swollen in the morning. Ron gave me a hug and encouraged me to keep writing. As for a baby? I was due to ovulate that week. Maybe I'd get pregnant on vacation.

❋

Ron and I went trail running on Sunday. Despite the summer heat, the mountain air was crisp and it turned our cheeks pink. On Monday, we rented bikes and pedaled up Snowball Road to Jackson Mountain. In the back woods at the river crossing, I raced through the water as Ron tried to capture the perfect action shot with his camera. We ended up with a memory stick full of blurry photos of my shirtsleeve. By that night, my anxiety began to dissipate. The truth was, I adored my husband and loved spending time with him. I was beginning to piece together a picture of what our future would look like without kids. Part of me would forever be sad over my infertility, but I had taken a step closer to letting go of the idea of Motherhood.

So on Tuesday morning, as I ate my breakfast of scrambled eggs, the last thing on my mind was adoption. Sipping a mug of tea, I was watching the birds out the window when the corner of my eye caught sight of my BlackBerry. The red message light was flashing. I clicked open the email: *Interested in adopting a little boy? It's a perfect case. The boy is in Honolulu. He's 15 months old. Private adoption. He's ready for a home.*

The woman who sent the email was a friend. She had inside information that the family who was supposed to adopt the boy had changed their minds at the last minute. If Ron and I were interested, my friend could connect us with the lawyer working on the case. My head immediately started buzzing. Yes, we were interested. Here was our Big Chance. We could adopt this baby. Love him and raise him.

Ron and I had explored the idea of adoption once before—even going so far as to complete a home study, an arduous process where a social worker vets prospective parents through a series of interviews, criminal background checks, and reference letters. But when we attended informational meetings at adoption agencies, or sat through RESOLVE support groups with other couples exploring adoption, the concept felt too nebulous. We never took the next step, and our paperwork lapsed.

Our last serious conversation about adoption had occurred three months before the email message showed up on my BlackBerry. Spring had just arrived in Washington, D.C., where Ron and I lived, and we were walking around the Tidal Basin taking in the cherry blossoms. It was cold outside, but sunny. The worn dirt path that circled the trees was swarming with parents and young kids. It made us mourn the baby I had miscarried, who would've been three years old. We broke away from the crowds and sat down on a low concrete wall. The topic of conversation turned to adoption. Do we or don't we?

"If we have our own kids, I'm sure," Ron said. "Adopting—I'm still ambivalent."

"Me, too," I said. I slipped off my mitten and held Ron's hand, looking for reassurance. I was ashamed of the way I felt. Parenting was parenting, wasn't it? What difference did it make if I birthed the baby or not? Were genes so important?

As if Ron was reading my mind again, he voiced my next thought. "We have the resources. We come from good families. It would be a nice thing to do."

It was true. We could provide. Food. Shelter. Safety. Finances. Education. Love. Did that obligate us to adopt? It felt selfish to turn away kids in need when we had been given so much.

"Somehow we have to decide," I said.

"The longer we do nothing, the more likely we'll stay on the de facto path of not adopting," Ron said.

For three months we did nothing. And then out of the blue, the BlackBerry message. The opportunity had taken us off-guard, but with an actual baby who could be in our arms within weeks, our interest in adoption reignited and skyrocketed. Ron and I called the lawyer working on the case. By that afternoon, we had copies of the baby's medical records, as well as profiles of his parents. We also had a photo. The little boy was adorable.

His name was Kai. He had huge, round eyes and dark hair. Milky white teeth poked out behind rosy lips. I liked the shape of his nose and ears. And best of all, he had my favorite skin color—that Pacific Island brown. The idea of adopting a baby of a different race had always appealed to me. To adopt a white child felt like we would be playing a game of Pretend (pretend I wasn't infertile; pretend the baby hadn't endured the trauma of being separated from its mother; pretend we were One, Big, Happy, Blood-Related Family). Kai's big brown eyes looked out at me from the screen, and I tried to picture him as our son.

According to the child psychiatrist who had examined him, Kai was behind developmentally, but there didn't appear to be anything to worry about. He could pull himself up, but he wasn't walking or talking yet. The doctor suspected that was due to a lack of parenting skills by his birth mother, a transient twenty-two-year-old who had been living with Kai on Hawaii's beaches before relinquishing him to foster care. When the psychologist had tested Kai's cognitive abilities, Kai laughed and clapped at the games. He quickly caught on that if he put blocks in the right slots, the toy would light up and play music. Kai's father was out of the picture. He and Kai's mom had met in a bar and had since broken up. And both of Kai's parents had signed consent forms giving their permission for an adoption.

"It's an open-and-shut case," the lawyer had told us.

It did seem ideal.

Except.

For reasons I couldn't figure out that day, I was frozen with indecision. I knew enough about adoption to know if Ron and I wanted this baby, we had to make a move. Fast. In America, the demand for healthy babies outweighs the supply. We called our social worker, who told us we'd have to start a new home study from scratch, but after a few more phone calls, we learned we could fork over some extra cash and complete an expedited home study in three weeks.

I asked Ron how he felt every two minutes.

Should we do this?

What do you think?

We sat outside on the deck and discussed it all day. I daydreamed about walking across Hawaii's lush green grass to meet Kai. Kneeling to look into his big, brown eyes. Playing with him on the sand with an oversized beach ball. Ron and I talked about logistics. Were we ready to halt the direction of our lives on a moment's notice and stock up on diapers, pacifiers, and wet wipes? We dissected the complicated issues surrounding adoption. Kai lived with his grandmother before the foster caretaker, so we would be his third placement. What about attachment disorder? Kai's birth mom wanted an open adoption so she could stay in contact with him. We thought that was a good thing—for Kai. But could we handle the confusing emotions an open adoption would entail?

The cabin deck overlooked thirty-five acres of wild earth. Land full of pine trees, untamed oak brush, junipers, and groves of aspens with their skinny, white trunks. It was a bird's haven, and as we watched them flit about, gathering food and chirping, Ron recalled a documentary on cowbirds he'd seen when he was seventeen. It had stuck with him all these years. Cowbirds drop their eggs in other birds' nests, abandoning their young and leaving them to be raised by adoptive parents. Many species kick the cowbird egg out of the nest (or cover the egg up), but some species, like warblers, raise the cowbird nestling, even to the detriment of its own fledglings.

"It doesn't add up," Ron said. "Why would the warbler mother, a small bird, run herself ragged feeding another bird's offspring?" He was moved by the tenderness of the warbler's actions and amused by the anomaly of nature.

Maybe it's ridiculous to compare the adoption of a human baby to the habits of birds, but in a way, it demonstrated how we felt. We'd be warblers raising a cowbird—someone else's child. And after wanting a baby for so long, I didn't understand why I didn't dart out of my chair, fly to Hawaii, and enfold Kai into my wings. Instead, I stayed suspended in a state of limbo, hesitating, like the hummingbirds hovering around us. What was wrong with me? Kai needed a mom and dad. Ron and I wanted to be parents. A baby was practically being handed to us. What better solution?

❄

For the next two days, I was a mess. One minute, I was excited, propping my laptop up on a countertop in the cabin so I could gaze at Kai's picture while I washed the dishes. As I soaped plates, I was positive we should adopt him. By the time I moved on to scrubbing the mugs, I was terrified. What did it mean to adopt?

When I was pregnant, I loved my baby—a blobby cluster of cells—immediately and fiercely. As the baby grew inside me, we were already bonding. My blood coursed through my system and pulsed into the baby's delicate heart. Even though the baby would have no conscious memory of being formed, he or she could sense the sound of my voice.

My breasts tingled and had begun to swell, and I looked forward to the day I would sit in a rocking chair and gaze into my child's face as I breast-fed. As the weeks passed, I placed my hand on my stomach and talked to the baby, mistaken in the belief that our relationship was just beginning, when in fact, it was about to end.

Would my love for Kai be that automatic? Would he fit with us and us with him? Or would we be mismatched puzzle pieces? I had heard accounts of adoptees that had sought out their biological parents later in life and felt like they were finally understood in a way they had never been before. In fact, every story I'd ever heard about adoption swam around in my head. I thought of my friend who had spiraled into depression after adopting. How the paperwork touted the child as healthy, but how he ended up having severe special needs. I thought of a lawyer I knew who adopted a daughter from Guatemala and had such a positive experience she wanted to adopt again. I thought of a mom who once told me her longing for a biological child never left, even after adopting two kids. And yet another who thought adopting was the best decision she'd ever made.

I thought of the movie starring Annette Bening *A Mother and Child* and the book *The Brotherhood of Joseph*. I remembered how my sister-in-law told me she sat on the floor with her screaming newborn, my nephew Noah, after coming home from the hospital. And how she thought about me and wondered how in the world I (or any woman) could tolerate the demands of new motherhood when the baby wasn't the child you had carried and birthed. I thought about how I loved Noah to pieces, and how nothing tickled me more than seeing traces of my brother in Noah's smiles and expressions. I thought about my friends—Debra and Christine—both adoptees and two of the most amazing women alive. How much I'd enjoy daughters exactly like them, blood-related or not. I knew that having a biological child was a mixed bag, just like adoption. But with adoption, something felt off.

Ron and I continued to talk, analyzing questions that drove us in loops. Ron wanted to defer to me (after all, I'd be taking on the bulk of child-rearing responsibilities). We went to bed without answers. When I bolted awake in the middle of the night, the questions still circled my mind, running centipedes. And they all boiled down to one thing: How badly did I want to be a mother?

"We don't have to decide anything now," Ron said when my tossing and turning woke him up.

But the truth was, we did have to decide. Maybe not at 3:00 AM, but at some point within the day or so. Who knew how many other families were jockeying for Kai?

Lying in bed, I realized I'd been spending all my time thinking about how the adoption would affect Ron and me. But what about Kai? How would he feel about having us as his parents? Kai deserved to be matched with a couple that wanted to adopt. Period. A couple that was bursting with desire to take him home. Until I was in that place, I knew we couldn't adopt Kai. When I finally drifted off to sleep, I was at peace with my decision. That is, until the next morning when my mom called.

Word about the potential adoption had seeped out among family and a few close friends.

"I think you should do it," my mom said.

And in that moment, I wanted to. I wanted to adopt Kai so my mom could be a grandmother. And because adopting Kai would make everyone else happy—the friends, siblings, and in-laws that had been waiting for Ron and me to join the ranks of parenthood. And society at large with its message that if I didn't stick with the storyline of marriage followed by motherhood, I would be less than. An outcast. A shame. So that morning, I questioned my sanity. Was I crazy? With a failing uterus, how many chances would Ron and I have to be parents?

My BlackBerry flashed again. The lawyer. She pressed us for a final answer. "I need to know," she said. "Otherwise, I have to make other arrangements."

All Ron and I had to do was send a text with two itty-bitty words: We're in. Two words that held so much weight and meaning, they would profoundly affect the rest of our lives. If we didn't answer within the hour, we'd lose Kai.

I didn't send the email.

I ovulated, but I didn't get pregnant.

Three months later, my uterus was gone. The organ was in a pathology lab, and I was in a hospital bed, still groggy from anesthesia, missing one body part. Recovering in the hospital room after my hysterectomy, I felt a pool of sadness inside me for the door that had been sealed shut.

As Ron fed me ice chips, I thought about the warblers and the cowbirds. The behavior of the warblers puzzled scientists for years. Eventually, scientists discovered that if the warbler failed to raise the cowbird chick, the cowbird mother, watching from a distant tree, would swoop in and destroy the warbler's nest. So the warblers were acting on animal instinct after all.

✺

For a long time I thought I'd failed to operate out of a higher level of consciousness by not adopting Kai. Hadn't I made the decision to stick with my primal urge for a genetic child? Reject another's young? Over time, I came to see that Ron and I had been faced with an emotionally gut-wrenching decision that needed to be made within days. The pressure was too intense. By not acting on a whim, we lost our chance to adopt Kai, but it was the only way I knew how to manage the decision. And in the time since, we have decided not to pursue adoption any further. We are a family of two, and we feel complete.

※

After I recovered from my hysterectomy, I began hosting an infertility support group through RESOLVE. Each month, I listened to women talk about how they decided to spend tens of thousands of dollars on advanced reproductive procedures, like in vitro fertilization, instead of using that money to pursue adoption. I sat with them as they cried over the loss of not being able to conceive a biological child, and the confusion they felt when admitting that a part of them wasn't okay with adoption, or with using donor eggs or donor sperm. I handed them tissues. Told them to take a breath. Reminded them that the path to Motherhood—or away from it—is different for everyone. That adoption is a choice and slowing down at a decisions crossroads is a good thing. And it's okay to make the choice not to adopt. To say out loud, "This doesn't feel right." There is no shame in that.

WHAT *Jenny* HOPES READERS WILL TAKE AWAY FROM HER STORY

"Wondering whether you'll feel differently about an adopted child verses a biological child is normal. Adoption is different. And when I say that, I don't mean it negatively—adoption can bring great joy and enrich lives. But adoption brings up complex issues and emotions. It's okay to acknowledge those and talk about them."

ELEMENTS OF SHAME
Kedren Werner

:

When the recession hit, it looked like I might squeak by with-out needing to get a job. I'd already scaled back. Called it my "Too Small to Fail" approach. A housekeeper from five days to two, gardeners from three days to one, pool cleaning to every other week, personal mainte-nance to zero. Even with my limited math skills, I knew that equaled me working all seven days. I was living within my means, if not following my bliss. When it looked like I was going to need a job, I told my sister and she said, "You're a tough sell on paper."

I have been a fashion model, an actress in a theater company, and a production executive. I was considered "full of potential," well posi-tioned to "become something," and "charismatic in a room." Attributes difficult to quantify on a resumé. Then I stopped working to stay home and parent my son. My attributes and ambitions were now channeled into my role as wife and mother: I reflected and furthered my husband's and son's accomplishments rather than my own. Some viewed me as a Trophy Wife. It never occurred to me that I would need to update my profile or refurbish myself with advance degrees and surgical enhancements. Like the new media, the platform I was delivered in was not that important as long as my content was worthwhile.

"I know," I said. "Even I wouldn't hire me."

Then my mom, who lives with me, was diagnosed with dementia. My anxiety with my inability to find my phone, keys, or purse was juxtaposed with the deeper grief for the loss of the mother I knew, of the grandmother my son adored and the only person other than myself to take care of him.

I have no regrets about the time I've spent taking care of James. As I like to say, the time we have with our children is short, but some days are really long. Yesterday was one of those days.

I was in the kitchen making dinner. In the little workroom off the kitchen, James was sitting at his desk. I could see him through the sliding glass door, hot-faced and tight-lipped. He had thrown all his paraphernalia—backpack, reusable lunch bag, and red P.E. shorts—on the floor near his chair. His toes gripped and ungripped the P.E. shorts as if he was kneading bread. He got up and slid the door open. Some Airsoft gun BBs had lodged in the tracks, so when he slid the door open it sounded like a train entering the station. He wore a light gray beanie low on his brow with the words *Snow Wonder* stitched above the fold. He received it years ago. A gift from a production in which my husband had given me a bit part so I could keep my health insurance. I remembered James asking me why I took the job. "You don't need a job. You already have one. I am your job."

I said, "Well, your job doesn't come with benefits."

Just as I was pouring olive oil into a skillet James stepped into the kitchen.

"I want to talk to you," he said.

"Okay, what about?"

I knew James wanted to talk about a long-term school project. Two weeks prior, he told me that his teacher had assigned the class a Family History Project. There are two different parents, he explained, so there are two different sets of history. It was up to James to determine how to present the narrative, and which side of the family to explore. Fundamental pieces of information were required to complete the assignment: where your family came from, why they left and came to America, and how that led to your birth and life in Los Angeles. As he read from the piece of paper, I felt myself become tired. This was one of those projects that was going to be time-heavy *for me*. I interrupted him.

"This is not an assignment," I said. "It's a concept letter. In order to find the assignment, you need to sit down with this." I gestured to the paper. "Cull through and extract the information your teacher is requiring from you out of this wish list."

He started to respond, "Yes. You're—"

"You need to do a complete task analysis," I interrupted. "Prioritize what you need to do so you can plan your time because I am not going to organize this—"

He continued, speaking in halting rhythms.

"—breaking up. I can't hear—"

"—and really use the two weeks to work on it because it's going to involve other people. . . ."

"Mom, hello? I can't hear you, bad connection."

We both laughed. "Are you pretending to be on a cell phone?" I said, "I get it. I get it." But I wasn't sure he did.

✴

My son's long-term assignments often end up being completed the night before they're due. Once he'd figured out what the assignment required, he'd get stuck. I would get him going again with a sensory jolt to the nervous system. I'd plead, yell, or even take over the project. James would be demoted to assistant project manager, offering up suggestions from the sidelines. But I didn't want to have that dynamic with him anymore.

When we got home my husband was there, home early from a television episode he was directing. During the twenty years we've been married, he has made a career out of wrangling divas. A few months ago, while we were folding laundry, my husband told me I was one of those divas.

"I don't know a lot of divas that do yard work," I said. "Or who give production notes on a screenplay, or pick up sewage from an overflow pipe." As he watched me refold the T-shirts he had just folded, he said, "Divas are extreme!"

My husband has various awards for his ability to observe behavior. I had to admit I fit his description.

We entered the exercise room. James sat on a large, yellow exercise ball in the coveted space next to his dad. "Tell Dad about the Family History Project," I said.

"Where did your family come from, Mom?" he asked me instead.

"Well," I said. "My dad was born in Santa Monica and my mom is from New Orleans."

"I know, but where were they from before that?" I didn't know the answer to that question.

So I went big picture and said, "I think you're going to find the families who are not of Anglo heritage will have vastly different answers to these questions than those that—"

"—I hope you're not going to be hurt or anything, but I'm pretty sure I'm going to do Dad's side of the family."

James came over, gave me a hug, and kissed the top of my head. I laughed and said, "I don't blame you. If I were you, I'd do your dad's side of the family, too."

My husband's family are descendants of Portuguese Jews who immigrated to America circa 1734. Their first-born son, Gershom Mendas Seixas, was the product of a "mixed" marriage: Sephardic-Ashkenazi Jews. Gershom was the first *chazzan* (minister) in the United States and, although not ordained, functioned as the rabbi for America's Jewish community. He even attended George Washington's inauguration to represent the Jewish population.

✴

My family is a lineage grab bag. The product of several "mixed" and perhaps not ordained marriages: African-American-Caucasian-French-Spanish and American Indian. I doubt that any of my relatives were at George Washington's inauguration, but if they were, they were working the party.

For the next two weeks, I occupied myself with things I'd been meaning to do for the last thirteen years. I sorted through bankers' boxes, our family time capsules, determined to make use of things. I glued statues for nominations that had not yielded awards to preschool woodwork projects, to make doorstops, and found other treasures not seen for a while. In a silk-lined woodcut box, there was a golden origami cup I'd made for my father when I was a little girl. It was wrapped in a note my dad had written excusing me from "sports" because "she does not feel up to par." The paper cup was faded in the folds where his fingertips held it and stained on the rim where he rested his lips to have a drink. When I tested it, it was still water-worthy. We had stood under the low-slung redwood beams of the carport when he handed me the note to take to school. I leaned into him and rested my head against his heart as he kissed the top of my head. "Love you, daughter," he said. "See you when I get home." The note was dated the day he died.

James was working on the project while I stayed out of his way. I hadn't asked even once, "How's the project coming?" Well, that's not true. I didn't ask straight out. I did it by making it about me. When I saw him with his headphones on, moving his head to "dubstep," I'd say, "I hope you're listening to the recording of your great grandmother's interview." When he was watching South Park with his dad, I'd pop in and say, "I hope you guys are talking about your project."

Then last night James gave my husband and me what he thought was his final draft of the Family History Project to read.

"This is embarrassing." I tossed the paper. The sheets separated and a couple of them fell to the floor. The contempt of the gesture held us captive like one of the pages trapped in a water ring. After a moment my husband retreated upstairs, James to his workroom, but I remained in the kitchen to prepare dinner. I knew James would come back and I knew what he'd want to talk about.

When James came in, he pointed to the little workroom.

"Mom, I want to talk to you in here."

After turning down the burner, I followed him in. He sat back down in his chair. I would have sat on the piano bench, but it was covered with piano books, guitar picks, and Legos. I knelt at his side instead.

James rolled the brim of the beanie up and adjusted it off the crown of his head so he could see me and I could see him better. "Mom," he said. "I'm sorry."

"Sorry for what?" I said.

"Sorry for letting you down."

I thought he was going to tell me that he'd learned his lesson about long-term assignments, understood why I was strict with him, and he was going to promise never to wait until the night before something was due to complete it. I was ready to console him about his project, but he was feeling bad about me because I was upset with him about his project. I wasn't prepared. I stood up. This Mother Mary at the foot of Jesus tableau wasn't good for what I had to say.

"Well that's where you're wrong. You're not letting me down," I said. "You're letting yourself down and that's the worst feeling of all, one I'm very familiar with."

He brought both of his hands to his forehead and pressed his palms to his temples until they were trembling from the pressure and said, "You say something about me, then it turns into something about you. There are so many levels of things going on, it's like (the movie) *Inception.*"

His elbows hit the desk with the full weight of his head in his hands. He stared down.

"Sometimes," he went on, "I think you want me to fail. You tell me, 'You're going to do this, you're not going to be able to do that, and then this will happen.' But you don't see how what you say makes me feel. You're like a mad scientist."

I was leaning over him and I took his hands in mine to pull him close to me, but I could not move him.

"When I have a son," he said, "I will never make him feel as worthless as you're making me feel right now."

I was shattered by his words. James had experienced my parenting methods for what they were, the diva mother approach. Much has been made of the Tiger Mom model of parenting versus the permissive Western model. I had been strict with James, but permissive with myself. I wanted Kant's Categorical Imperative graded on a curve. The imperative states: "Act as if your actions will become a universal law." But I wanted how I acted to be universal law only when I was the one acting that way. I would have hated to be treated as I'd treated him. Appalled if he took my behavior as a model, I had been patronizing and punitive, rather than supportive and invested in his process as a student.

I thought to say, "I know how you feel," but didn't. My son is a descendant of my husband and me: a mixed marriage of my husband's kind nature, his blue eyes, and lean fingers. But my son's sense of worthlessness is an element from my periodic table. It occurs as naturally in me as the first ninety-four chemical properties occur on earth. It is arranged in the same row as guilt and regret, opposite pride, above pity and aimlessness, its valence number perfectly suited to bond with avoidance and fear.

I had taken something genetically predisposed and nurtured it—created the very thing I'd set out to prevent—I wanted James to feel accomplished, but the way I went at it left him feeling unsure of his own innate abilities. When did I lose the ability to nurture my son's sense of his own capability?

When did my life get so small, my capacity so limited, that I had to make this young boy the container for my unrealized dreams?

When did my potential, "the most elastic of human qualities," get stretch marks? I had tried to do the impossible: raise someone to have a fulfilling life and therefore make my life fulfilling. I saw myself as one of my homemade doorstops, a tarnished Trophy Wife stuck to my son's old school projects, holding open doorways, blocking them a bit, while trying to make use of myself. But you cannot use what you do not value.

I value my career, but I am ashamed I didn't do more with it. I value institutional learning, but I am ashamed that I am self-taught. I value beauty, but I am ashamed that I have lost my looks. I value intellect, but I am ashamed that my thinking is clouded. I value accomplishment, but I am ashamed mine are not greater. I value family, but I am ashamed I don't know my history. I value my marriage, but I am ashamed I do not express enough love for my husband. I value my son, but I am ashamed that I make him feel worthless. Somewhere along the line, I decided I would not be able to achieve my goals or be what I valued. I made my goals smaller, my life smaller, too small to succeed.

My parents used to counsel me, "What you do not bring to consciousness becomes your fate." Shame can lead to more shame. My shame about my own unrealized potential led to behavior toward my son that left me more ashamed. I wasn't seeing my son, I was seeing instead myself—all struggles and failures, all half-hearted attempts, all my diminishments. Of course I flung the papers across the table. I was flinging myself as far from myself as possible. I was ashamed of what I was seeing, not of my son, but of myself. My shame had led to more shame, manifest not only in me but also in my behaving in a way that made my son ashamed of himself. James experienced the difficulty of my struggle, not the grit it takes to engage with it. And in my struggle with worthiness, I am not inert. I struggle every day to do better, to be grateful, to connect, and to be seen, flaws and all.

Like that origami cup, when I am tested, I am still water-worthy. That's my content. That's my value. That's my strength. I want James to know it's okay to be stuck, we all are, but we are built for challenges. We are resilient. We are determined. It's part of my lineage. It's what I have passed down to him from the generations of my family that led to my birth and my life in Los Angeles with my husband and my son. I want him to experience the satisfaction of hanging in there even when he doesn't feel "up to par." Teaching him that is my job—one that comes with amazing benefits. And if it means getting another job to do that one well, I will. Life is a long-term project and I have not been doing enough work to be ready to proceed with my narrative.

It is time for my own project, to deal with my own history of inadequacy. To journey from the country where my currency is devalued, and make a newly minted life in this undiscovered country of my own being. I knew that this journey would expose the gap between my reality and my ideal. Be a place I experienced suffering. My potential would be realized in working to close that gap. But it mattered where I focused that effort. I started where I was. In the little workroom off the kitchen I leaned into my son, rested his head on my heart, kissed the top of his head and said, "No, I'm the one who's sorry."

RESIDUAL SHAME
Colleen Haggerty

:

"Hey, Colleen, some of us are taking a walk downtown. Wanna come?" My heart leapt when Cecilia asked me to go with her and some of the girls from our dorm floor, but I felt dread. I was dying to make new friends since college started four weeks previous, but I wasn't sure I could walk downtown and back.

"Sure, I'll come." The words popped out before I could think. Everyone walked downtown. It was only a mile and a half. How could I admit that for me it seemed like ten miles? As I grabbed my coat I felt excited to be invited and nervous that my leg would hurt too much and I wouldn't be able to keep up. Although these girls knew I was an amputee—they had all seen me in shorts; they'd seen me hop out of the shower on one leg in our communal bathroom—but up until then we had only sat around in our rooms talking. They were about to see how limited I really was.

Nine months before, I had been in a car accident that cut off my leg above the knee. I recovered quickly and was able to finish high school on time. While I was grateful for my prosthetic leg, it was a clunky, heavy piece of plastic and wood I lugged around with me all day and it gave me a distinctive limp.

Six of us loaded into the elevator before we encountered our first series of steps leading outside. I took each of the five steps one at a time, like a little kid.

"Do you need help?" Cecilia asked.

"No, thanks, I've got it." While part of me was grateful that she was looking out for me, I wished I wasn't in the position to ever need help.

The walk downtown started on a downhill slope which requires a different gait than level ground, so I kept my head down and concentrated on each step. My brow started to sweat.

"Have you met Brian in 311? He is so cute, but I swear he's a pothead." Amy was talking to Cecilia. Their conversation faded into the background as I focused on each step.

Enid slowed down and fell in step with me. "Do you have Professor Jensen, Colleen?"

"No, I don't," was all I could manage through my heavy breathing. I felt the familiar discomfort of my prosthetic leg, making it hard for me to engage in chitchat.

"Well, she is such a bitch. Do you know she makes us take a pop quiz once a week? I can't believe it. It's so unfair. I should just drop the *blah blah blah.* . . . ."

I couldn't listen anymore, except to the leaves crunching underfoot. The friction between my prosthetic leg and my crotch rubbed a raw spot. I could tell a blister was starting to form.

This is so stupid. Why did I come on this walk anyway? I fought back the tears. I wanted to throw up.

❋

The sidewalks downtown were crowded. *Outta my way!* I wanted to scream at the people walking toward me. I glared at anyone who forced me to alter my gait. A scowl burrowed its way deep into my brow, I was so focused on walking through each painful step. The other girls left me alone; they could tell I was in pain. All I wanted was to be happy, to make a joke, to feel connected. Instead my anger was like a force field repelling people away from me. I was blowing it.

After a short reprieve at a café, we started our walk back to the dorm. The pain increased with each step. As we neared the dorm, we had to climb the hill we walked down at the beginning. I lagged behind the rest of the girls; no one seemed to notice. I resented them and their perfect two-legged bodies. I resented their laughter as they walked with such ease. I resented that they left me behind.

My skin was prickling from the heat of the walk and the shame of my limitations being so starkly revealed. I acted like a bitch. I couldn't contain my fury—it oozed out of every pore in my body. I wondered what the girls thought of me now.

My eyes start to blur. *NO! I won't let myself cry.* I wiped my runny nose with my sleeve and kept limping up the stupid hill. I shouldn't have come.

Back at our dorm, I walked up the stairs one at a time, like a toddler. I opened the door to my room and fell on my bed, exhausted.

The tentacles of pain weren't limited to my stump; they reached throughout my body, over to my good leg, up to my lower back, and up even farther, to my heart, leaving it with the heaviness of shame.

✳

I had to learn a new way to be in the world after my accident. Before my amputation, I was a fairly quiet person. Without meaning to, I often faded into the background. If there's anything that puts a person front and center, it's a prosthetic leg. I lived in a fishbowl: People seemed to watch my every move. I didn't have any experience being so visible.

While others saw strength and courage in me, I grappled with the humiliation of my limitations. I lost my leg just as the jogging movement was getting its own legs. I felt like an imposter when I was in a circle of friends talking about their best running time or distance, like a pauper at a princess's wedding. I adopted the belief that because I was not whole physically, I wasn't enough.

In my twenties I pushed at the edges of my true limitations. I dabbled in sports and activities and found a few that I both loved and was capable of doing: backpacking, skiing, and sea kayaking.

Some of my limitations were physical. The farthest I could walk with a backpack, for instance, was five miles—and that was a push. The few friends I hiked with learned to give me space so I could spend time with myself on the trail. I turned inward and focused on each step. I took my time.

Other limitations were mental. When I kayaked in high winds, fear got in my way, not my prosthetic leg. I was afraid of drowning, since that was how I'd lost my father, who had died on a fishing trip when I was just thirteen years old. Fighting the fear often took just as much energy as managing the physical pain.

Engaging in activities that pushed my limits seemed to compensate for my deficits. I deceived myself, and I deceived others; my participation in these activities made me appear normal.

*

When I was finishing my BA degree in recreation in my mid-twenties, after a three-year hiatus from college, our class went to Mount Baker for a backpacking trip in the snow. Ron, our professor, checked in with me prior to the trip to ask if I could manage the hike; I assured him I could. I felt a little cocky, being a seasoned backpacker. At twenty-six, I was one of the oldest of the group and already felt a slight distance between my classmates and me, who were mostly in their early twenties, fit and active.

I didn't anticipate how hard it would be to hike in the snow. I don't remember the hike up; it was the hike back down, a few days later, which left an emotional scar in my memory.

The nemesis of anyone wearing a prosthetic leg is ice. On the hike down the trail, I found myself walking on a sheet of it. Each step I took was precarious; I never knew if or when I was going to fall. Prosthetic knees are unreliable in these situations. Bearing weight on it while it's bent makes the knee collapse. I took baby steps, hunched over like a fearful old lady. All that was missing was a walking stick. Since it was winter, I couldn't even find one on the side of the trail. I was left to my own limited devices. Ron took up the back of the group, there to herd along any strays that wandered. I was the sickly sheep, lagging behind the rest of the flock.

After half a mile of traversing the hillside, my prosthetic leg suddenly slipped from under me. I landed with a thud onto my backpack. Both the sudden shock of the fall and the impact left me breathless. It took a few seconds to realize what had happened and when I did my face flushed with embarrassment. I quickly looked to the trail ahead and saw a few of my classmates turn around to check out the noise. I immediately looked away, mortified. Ron offered me his hand. He hefted me up and we continued to walk hand in hand.

I had boasted about my successes in the wilderness—assured him that I could handle it. The other students were far ahead; hell, some of them were surely already back at the bus. I would learn later in life that anger usually masks an underlying emotion. The rage that seeped out of me that day, I now know, was shame. I wanted desperately to be one of the gang. I hungered for the acceptance. I didn't want to be singled out because of something that I wasn't even ready to call a disability yet. In my shame I'd grown to hate my body. Instead of being proud of my accomplishments, I could only focus on what I couldn't do, where I fell short, and how my body had betrayed me.

Ron and I didn't speak the whole way down. I just held onto his hand, bearing weight on him as we navigated every step. I stifled the tears and tried to hold back my rage. My throat burned from my stifled screams.

I took a deep breath before climbing the stairs up into the bus, knowing my classmates would be there watching me. *Just get it over with.* As soon as I got to the top step they started to clap, smiles on their faces. One look at the scowl on my face and their sudden outburst died a quick death. I limped to an empty seat and sat down with a thud. People in nearby seats muttered praise, "Hey, great job, Colleen," but I couldn't respond. Resentment and anger seeped out of me like a scared skunk filling the air with its putrid, acrid scent, warding off everyone around me. I saw them shrink back with confused looks that I could only interpret as pity.

What was so easy for them had been tortuous for me. They acted as a mirror, reflecting back to me everything that had been taken from me when I was hit by that car. Their praise didn't feel encouraging, it felt condescending. I was twenty-six years old and I was being commended for walking two miles in the snow?

My experience with being disabled is that there is a fine line between being admired and being condescended to. What can the world expect of an amputee and how much did I exceed those expectations? When I rose above them, I could accept praise or admiration. When I fell below, the praise and admiration felt patronizing. After that hike in the snow, I felt like my classmates were trying to take care of me. Couldn't they see that their kindness only made things worse? After exposing my vulnerabilities, both my physical limitation and my emotional immaturity, I was afraid of being judged as less than—so afraid, in fact, that I beat them to the punch. I clung hard to the belief that I wasn't good enough. The loneliness this inflicted was a weight far heavier than my prosthetic leg, and I carried it with me for years.

❄

It took time for me to work through the shame of my limitations and the anger that so often overlaid it. I became artful in controlling situations so that I appeared successful. I continued backpacking, kayaking, and skiing, but I did those activities on my terms, taking control where I could or, at the very least, deciding with whom I did the activities.

I set a boundary around my physical abilities for the first time when I was part of a women's group in my early thirties. The group had decided (during a week I was away) that we were going to take a walk during our meetings. When they told me the plan, I fell silent. *How do I tell them I can't walk every meeting? How can they be so insensitive to assume I can?* I was used to controlling situations so that I looked competent, but I suddenly found myself out of control.

At the start of our next meeting, I spoke up and admitted to the women that I wouldn't be able to do the walk. They were shocked; given all the other activities I did, they assumed I could walk. I couldn't believe it. I was surprised that I *had* passed myself off as normal when I'd been living in isolated fear that I couldn't pull that off. They assumed walking was easy for me when, in fact, it was—and continues to be—one of the biggest challenges of my life. I was also confused. If they saw me as normal, yet I saw myself as lacking and not whole, then who was right? I had spent years trying to make my disability a nonissue to others; I was just beginning to understand how big of an issue it was for me.

Over the years I've become more adept at setting boundaries for myself and stating my limits. I'm actually proud when I do because I'm taking care of myself. But I still feel the sting of shame from having an imperfect body. That I cannot do one of the most basic of physical functions—walking—is a struggle for me, as is how much my limitations impact others. I feel responsible that my weakness affects other people's experience.

The older I get, the less I care about what other people think of my limitations. I've learned to shift my self-deprecation into self-acceptance. I've discovered how my amputation is a strength even in its weakness. I've learned that the messages I tell myself about who I am are far more powerful than the judgments I fear from others.

WHAT *Colleen* HOPES READERS WILL TAKE AWAY FROM HER STORY

"Aside from relating to my story, I want my story to inspire questions for the reader. Where do I need to set more boundaries? How much of my life is spent taking care of others? How much shame do I feel about my body in general or a certain part of my body? We can become so used to our blinders, we don't even know we're wearing them. I hope my story can help readers see beyond their shame."

MATCHING RAINBOWS
Laurenne Sala

⋮

When I was three, my father left.

Divorce wasn't yet a popular pastime in our small Chicago suburb, so people talked. Snickered, maybe. There were whispers at PTA meetings and raised eyebrows in the bread aisle.

If that weren't bad enough, mine were the oldest parents on the block. My friends' moms swung ponytails and listened to Whitesnake. My mom had short hair and belted The Temptations songs from her Pontiac. Now, I can see what a blessing it is to have a mom who has lived before motherhood. But, then. Then, I was mortified. I lived on the "wrong" side of town in a house with my single, older mother. I wore Kmart clothes and didn't know how to French-braid my hair. All my friends had two parents and shopped at cool stores in the mall. It's funny how we classify people when we're young: where they shop, where they live, whether they can braid their hair. I failed in all three. I felt like an outsider, an outlier, an inferior crumb. And then, at eleven years old, I learned the real reason my parents had divorced eight years before: My dad left her for a man. A *man!*

And all that time, I just thought he was European. Really. He was a tall Spaniard who carried a man-purse way before they were in style. This news about his sexuality froze me. I didn't judge it. Instead, I felt betrayed. I'd spent eight years meeting my dad's boyfriends, not knowing they were boyfriends. I'd spent several consecutive Gay Pride parades marching because "Dad wanted to support his friends from work." My mom took me to the Holiday Inn to come clean, and I stared at the vomit-colored carpeting and felt so alone. I couldn't trust my own parents. Or any adults. And I definitely couldn't trust my friends. Junior high friends aren't really familiar with unconditional love. They gossip and backstab. They have secret notebooks and invite-only parties. I couldn't let them know how different I really was. And, really, I was.

Different. And alone. I could only count on myself. And since I was such a weirdo, I found that to be a shitty deal.

Today, gay parents are more accepted (in blue states), but in 1994 homosexuality was just recently off the APA's list of mental disorders. I loved my dad. I loved to dance on his feet. I loved that he took more time to wrap gifts than he did to pick them out. I loved his summer white pants and how he always fell asleep in the sun. I loved the musky scent of cigarettes and leather that swirled about his car. I loved his sarcasm and his cynical view of the world. I supported my dad. I never thought him weird for being gay. Him, I was able to accept. But accepting myself wouldn't happen for fifteen more years. I made my father's sexuality about me, about how much I stood out from the "normal" people.

Different hair and a single mom: That was one thing. But this. This was big. This was *not* normal. At school, I wouldn't let anyone know about my father. I couldn't. The word *fag* bounced around the junior high halls regularly, and I didn't want to come near it. For a girl who wanted nothing more than to be just like everyone else, telling my truth was not a possibility. One more weird thing about me, and they'd cross me off the list. I'd be relegated to the cafeteria corner with the band nerds.

Shame filled my lungs and poured from my pores. Shame for my family, me, and my entire existence. I had to always be alert, protecting my double life so that nobody would find me out. I would watch my father sing baritone in the Chicago Gay Men's Chorus on weekends and then spend the week panicking that someone might find out. If my father ever came to school, I would beg him to not look "gay." I alternated between smiles: One was real and one was full of anxiety.

And then, when I was sixteen, my father left again.
This time, it was much worse than divorce.
This time, forever.

It was suicide. Death by intention.
Gone. Goodbye. *Won't see ya later.*

He had been at war with depression since he could remember. After he closed his business, he let his depression win. Entrenched in his own self-hatred, he hid in his apartment, found comfort only in bottles of scotch, and berated himself until he couldn't take it anymore.

He left a note addressed to me, assuring me it wasn't my fault, but I didn't believe him. I remember our last conversation. I had been on the phone with a popular boy when he called.

"Dad, can I call you back? I'm on the other line."

I guess you always remember the last words. *I'm on the other line.*

My father spent most of his life hiding from people. When he finally came out as himself, I asked him to hide. How could I have done that? How could I have made that popular boy I was talking to more important than my dad? I was sure that if I had let him be himself around me, he wouldn't have made The Decision. If I had just called him back, he wouldn't have done it. If I had only been better/more normal, he wouldn't have wanted to leave me. He would have felt like I wanted him to be there. He would have wanted to be there.

But I hadn't let him feel that. I let shame kill my father.

※

I could have learned from his death that being authentic is the answer and that acceptance is freeing. I could have joined a support group. I could have learned that suicide is nobody's fault. I could have stopped to notice that I was only sixteen and couldn't have controlled my father even if I had tried.

But I was too ashamed to claim it. I didn't talk about it. How could I? People don't respond well to "he killed himself" when they ask about your dad. They apologize. They backpedal. They think back to previous parts of the conversation, wondering if they've made any jokes about wanting to die.

So, when I went to college, I changed my story. To my new friends, my dad lived in Europe. Or he died of a brain tumor. Or he had a crazy run-in with a roller coaster. Nobody knew the truth, because nobody knew me.

My self-hatred grew like a fungus. I let suicide and guilt stain me on the inside while alcohol kept me fun on the outside. I was still on a quest to be normal, and I must have thought "crazy drunk girl" seemed more acceptable than "girl whose dad didn't care to see her get married." I guess in our society, that's still the hierarchy. So I got drunk. I did plenty of drugs, the kind that make you forget. I said *yes* more than I wanted. I had sex more than I should have. I glided through life slathered in secrets, much like my father probably did.

Seven years after college, I started studying Buddhism. I realized that life is full of suffering and that I could *choose* to either suffer along or learn from it. In a monastery in Thailand, it finally hit me: If I continued to agonize and hide and see only my negative parts, I was no different than my dad. I loved my dad. I missed my dad. I would have given anything to talk to my dad. To apologize. To sit on his lap. To listen to his long scientific explanations of *The Simpsons* plots. But I didn't want to be *like* him. I was sure of that. I didn't want to end up alone on a futon with a plastic bag over my head.

❋

On Father's Day 2010, fourteen years after he died, I started writing about him. I let my fingers have free reign and there he was in my words. I dug around for every memory and wrote it out. I wrote about his gift-wrapping and his leather coat and his sexuality. I wrote that I accepted him fully and loved him. I pressed SUBMIT and published it on the Internet. Immediately, responses filled my inbox. Strangers reached out to tell me they cried and that I inspired them to accept their parents. I felt it was my duty to tell them everything, so I wrote about his suicide, too. I told the whole damn story, the one I'd held inside for fourteen years. I clicked SUBMIT again. And again. And again. And I was finally free. I sat there on my couch as tears met my keyboard and cried and cried. Loud. Fat. Tears. Big ones. I had come out now. After fourteen years of hiding, it was my turn to come out. Unlike my father, I knew I had a *choice* to live happily no matter what the response. I was choosing to no longer define myself by what other people thought of me.

I loved that feeling of relief so much that I wanted to share it with more people. I started a storytelling show called Taboo Tales. It encourages others to share their stories on stage, stories they've been holding in, stories of incest or breast cancer or HIV. Stories that would make most society members backpedal. Stories that have always been on the tips of tongues but have burrowed back in fear. Stories like mine. My favorite part is the hugs from strangers afterward.

Acceptance.

If I got a do-over, of course I would call my dad back. I would call every five minutes. I would sew us both matching rainbow flag outfits that read, "My DAD is a FAG, and I love him more than anything!"

But I don't think about do-overs anymore (okay, maybe sometimes). I think about what I have now and am grateful for every bit of it. If my father hadn't fallen down the well of depression, I don't know who I would be today. And I really love who I am today. Finally. Maybe that sounds funny—like I'm happy to have had a dad who suffered and languished. That's not true. But I am happy to have a life from which I can learn. My father still happens to be one of my greatest teachers.

WHAT *Laurenne* HOPES READERS WILL TAKE AWAY FROM HER STORY

"We're all hiding something until we're honest. And honesty frees us up to be who we are."

THE LAST SECRET
Amy Wise

⋮

"Mama, do you believe in abortion?"

My daughter Tatiana and I had talked about pretty much everything during her seventeen years, but this was one topic we never discussed. I always made sure the conversations veered around it. Now here I was, standing in the middle of our kitchen, posed with the question. I stuttered and stammered, "Oh, uh . . . that's a tough one. There's so much more to it . . . um . . . than you know . . . just believing in abortion." Before I could answer her, mercifully, the phone rang. Tatiana went about her business and I never had to address the question I had avoided for so many years.

What she didn't ask me, thankfully, was if *I* had ever had an abortion.

If we had finished that conversation in the kitchen, not only would I have shared my personal belief on abortion, but it would have been the *right* time to reveal my long-held secret.

When I was a senior in high school, about to head off to college with my boyfriend, Mark, I found out I was pregnant. My first reaction was denial. How could this be? We thought we were careful. I started getting a belly fairly fast because I was tall and thin and adding even one pound to my frame was obvious. I was also an exercise nut so gaining weight just didn't make sense. My mom asked me if I had stopped doing my sit-ups. I think that was her *roundabout* way of getting to the *truth*. I flippantly said I was taking a break and moved on. I wondered if my parents knew and were in just as much denial as I was.

On graduation day as I walked down the aisle to get my diploma, nobody but Mark knew. What should have been a joyful time instead was filled with fear. I left immediately after graduation and attended summer session, now able to deal with my confusion in silence. I was surrounded by thousands of people, yet felt totally alone as I walked the campus tortured by my secret.

Mark and I knew we had to decide soon. There is a very small window before it's too late and time was not on our side. It was a difficult decision, but we came to the conclusion that abortion was the only answer for us. Now we had to figure out how to get it done.

✻

Our college was in a tiny town so it would have to be done in the city. Not only were we dealing with emotional and financial issues, but my Dad was a surgeon and knew most of the doctors in town. I worried about word getting back to my parents through my Dad's colleagues. Privacy laws would not have allowed that, even back then, but rational thinking is not something that occurs when dealing with such a heartbreaking decision.

I finally found a doctor that didn't know my dad, or at least I assumed he didn't. Either way, I convinced myself I was in the clear. We made an appointment and days later we drove to the city to get *it* done. I was scared. Sad. Horrified.

We were silent as we took the two-hour drive from school to the city. Mark reached over to hold my hand, but I didn't want him to touch me. I pushed him away. I was hurt and angry that I had to go through this and all he had to do was drive. My mind was racing as fast as the car and I didn't *see* anything but a blue blur of sky. I rocked back and forth in the front seat wishing I could crawl into a hole and never come out.

We finally arrived at the office. I felt like everyone was staring and judging me. I went to the front desk and the receptionist was surprisingly kind as she handed me the clipboard and pen with the required paperwork attached. After I filled out the forms, a counselor asked me to come to her office. I sat down and she explained how the procedure worked and told me what to expect. Then she asked all the typical questions, "Are you sure you want to do this?" I said, "Yes." "Is this your decision?" "Yes." More questions, "Blah, blah, blah." "Yes, yes, yes."

I was numb.

I didn't hear her.

I just wanted to disappear.

But . . . *this was my choice*, for me, us. For the future I, we, had planned.

⚙

The receptionist called my name and my stomach turned. The nurse asked me to follow her to an exam room. She gave me a blue paper gown. She left. I changed and waited for the inevitable. I sat on the cold, vinyl exam table, my legs dangling, hoping they would forget me. The nurse walked me to *the room* and had me lie down on the table. I turned off my brain, shut down my heart, and closed my eyes as tears rolled down both sides of my face. From that moment on, I don't remember a thing. I chose to be put under anesthesia during the abortion. I counted backward and was out.

When I woke up, for just a moment, I forgot where I was and why. Then, sadly, I remembered. The nurse came to my bedside and said there was a handsome young man waiting to see me. She had a smile on her face. Most of the girls were there alone. I should have felt lucky that I had someone by my side. I didn't. It was the loneliest moment of my life.

Mark held my hand and asked if I was okay.

I answered with an emphatic *No!*

I was in terrible pain. I felt I deserved it. Now what? Was I just supposed to go on?

✸

After my time in the recovery room we got in the car and took the two-hour drive back to college. I cried the entire time. Mark tried to talk to me but I needed silence to grasp what *we* had just done. When we got back to campus, we went to his apartment and I fell to the floor with the worst cramps I had ever experienced. I thought I was going to die. Horrible thoughts ran through my mind as the pain pulsated through my body. I curled up in a ball, sobbing, bleeding, and broken. I was being punished for my choice. I decided then and there I would never tell anyone. I would bury this secret *forever.*

As time went on, I didn't think I would ever have children. I wasn't sure if I deserved them after what I did, or if I just wasn't meant to be a mom. Maybe it was both. I had zero maternal feelings and couldn't picture children being a part of my life. How could they be after what I had done?

During my junior year of college, I went overseas to study in Paris for a semester. When I got back, Mark proposed to me. A year later, we were married. Five short years after that, we divorced. Let's just say he had a *loose* definition of vows. I think we were doomed from the start. The abortion started our future off on a negative note and it just went downhill from there. It wasn't the cause of our demise, but it certainly didn't help. After the divorce, I had no desire to get married again and felt even stronger about not wanting children.

I was doing my thing when life, as it often does, decided to make its own plans.

※

In 1992, two years after my divorce, I met Jamie, the love of my life. After dating for only a couple of months, we knew we wanted a future together. We shared everything with each other. There were no secrets. I told him about my abortion and there was no judgment, only understanding. From the moment we fell in love, I knew I wanted to have a family with him. All my doubts about having children melted away. I could never picture having children with Mark because family wasn't his priority . . . *he* was his priority. With Jamie, family is his heart, and that is what changed mine.

Jamie and I were married in 1993. Our beautiful daughter Tatiana was born a little over a year later. I loved being a mom.

I was meant to be a mom.

Jamie and I have been married for nineteen years now and our family is my treasure. Jamie is black and I am white so trials and tribulations would be an understatement. We have dealt with many ups and downs, but remain strong through it all.

Years after I had Tatiana, I went to the doctor with terrible pain and heavy bleeding. He looked at me and said, "I'm so sorry to have to tell you this because you are so young, but you're going to need an emergency hysterectomy." I thought *he* was going to cry. He asked if Jamie and I wanted more kids and was pleasantly surprised when I told him we decided to have only one child and were perfectly happy with our family.

But I was terrified at the thought of surgery. So many thoughts went through my mind. This was probably happening because of the abortion I had so many years ago. I must have torn up my insides. More punishment, more guilt, more shame. I was still hanging on to what I had done so many years before. Would I ever forgive myself?

Why didn't I choose adoption? I, myself, *was adopted*. . . . If my biological mom had chosen abortion there would be no *me*. I've always thought that adoption was such an incredible, unselfish gesture. Although I was given away, and had a great life, I couldn't imagine giving my child away to someone else. Was I selfish?

The decision my eighteen-year-old self made felt right.

❉

I finally found the courage and told Tatiana about my abortion. I knew it was time. We were driving home from a mother/daughter day at the mall and I said, "I have something to tell you."

She looked at me, "You're scaring me. What?"

I apologized to her for keeping a secret. And then I started to talk.

She turned to me with wide eyes. "What!? I'm shocked!" Then . . . silence.

I looked over at her as I was driving, "Are you okay?"

"I never imagined you ever having an abortion." She started to cry.

And then the floodgates, tears pouring down both of our faces.

Tatiana turned and said, "Mama, it's okay to cry. You did what you had to do at the time. It's okay."

In an instant, twenty-nine years of weight lifted off my shoulders. I had no more secrets. We talked some more. She opened up and shared about some of her friends that have had abortions and how hard it was for them. It was intense. We arrived home, got out of the car, and hugged. Without needing to say a word, we just held on to each other.

I still needed to share this with my parents. I finally got the strength to do it on a recent visit back home. They had no idea. My mom cried, and said, "It must have been so hard to go through that without us." I didn't feel judged, I didn't feel shame . . . I just felt love and relief. That is the thing about shame; we tend to put it on ourselves.

At forty-seven years old, I am done holding in the hurt. I am proud of the woman I have become. I believe with all my heart that I am the mama I am today because of the mom I couldn't be back then. If Tatiana came to me today and told me she was pregnant, I would be there to listen and I would respect her choice.

Abortion is one of the hardest things to go through. However, a woman's body is something that can't be *legislated*. Every woman has the right to freedom of choice. Just as it was my biological mother's choice to give me away for adoption, it was my choice to have an abortion. My life. My choice.

We all make mistakes.

My past molded my present.

I have no regrets, only lessons learned.

WHAT *Amy* HOPES READERS WILL TAKE AWAY FROM HER STORY

"I want my story and every story in this book to give people hope that no matter how difficult things might get, we should never feel shame. With love and support we can make it through anything, together."

STINKIN' SHAME
Robyn Hatcher

⋮

"Mm, mm, mm, that's a stinkin' shame!" was a common chorus in the songs of my childhood. Depending on the tone and the conversation, it could convey sympathy: "So-and-So's husband just lost his job." *"Mm, mm, mm,* that's a stinkin' shame"—meaning the speaker liked So-and-So and was sorry she was having a hard time. The phrase could also be used to show empathy and be expressed seriously or humorously. But the tone that really shaped and affected my sense of self and draped me in a shroud of shame was the one spoken in hushed, guttural tones. This tone conveyed the more literal meaning of the words. That tone seemed to be reserved for whenever an African American individual was caught doing something stupid, violent, or otherwise shameful. *"Mm,*

mm, mm that's a stinkin' shame"—meaning: That fool just set back the whole black race.

Watching the evening news was a breeding ground for the Stinkin' Shame Chorus. I grew up in the sixties and seventies, a time when news reporting was taken more seriously. News anchors were authorities; they were the arbiters of what was good and right and what was bad and wrong. And almost every evening at 6:00 PM a similar scenario took place in my family. An intelligent-looking Caucasian reporter (because they were all intelligent-looking back then—and Caucasian) recounted a story about an armed robbery, a riot, a murder, arson, or some other horrific crime. We often watched TV with my mother's family—aunts, uncles, grandmother. We sat silently as details of the news story unfolded. (You have to understand, silence in this family was a *very* rare occurrence.) They were waiting, anticipating the moment when the photo splashed across the screen. If the perpetrator was black, there was guaranteed to be at least one utterance of the Stinkin' Shame Refrain. Sometimes the whole choir sang it. My grandmother was the lead singer. She had a way of saying the word *stinkin'*—deep, dark, and from the very back of her throat—that made it sound like a thousand tons of vile excrement or hundreds of gallons of putrefied garbage was hurling down on the heads of every black person in America. Other comments erupted afterward, about how awful, crazy, stupid, ridiculous the crime or person was. And how awful, crazy, stupid, ridiculous, and embarrassing (read: shameful) black people were. (I did mention we were black, right?) My family had a very confusing way of talking about black people as though we weren't in the room.

If the perpetrator of the crime turned out *not* to be black, there was an audible sigh of relief, often punctuated with someone saying what everyone else was thinking, "Thank God he wasn't black."

This, I believe, was the origin of both my shame about my racial identity and my aversion to watching or reading the news. It wasn't until the 2008 election of the first black president that I realized how much shame I had been carrying.

※

Where does shame begin? Is it learned? Is it inherited? Can it start with one event or does it need a series of events? Did my shame begin during those evening news hours or had the seed been sown many years before on some long ago plantation or slave ship, or because of some other family humiliation? Would my shame while watching the news have been mitigated had there been more positive images of African Americans in the media? Would my shame have existed if my mother hadn't striven for "the best" for us? The best neighborhoods, the best schools, the best opportunities—resulting in her choosing neighborhoods, schools, and opportunities that happened to be mostly white. Which translated to me: Black = bad. White = good.

Wherever and whenever the shame began, I spent most of my life denying that it existed. I wanted to believe that my having mostly white friends, a white husband, and white social conventions had nothing to do with shame. It was just how things worked out and there was nothing wrong with it.

I wasn't in complete denial. I knew I had issues. I had constant reminders of those issues. My own sister several years ago asked me if I had *any* black friends. (I did!) My sister, being three years older, hadn't translated the messages my family sent in the same way as I did. Or maybe she did, but, as with most things, decided to rebel against them, while I took them as gospel.

I distinctly remember being about seven or eight, alone in my room ruminating over the issue of race. I was trying very hard to figure out why some people were born white and some were born black. And most important, I was trying to figure out why I was "chosen" to be born black. I was a good Catholic girl at the time and believed that God must have made these choices for a reason.

As I was ruminating, I had an epiphany. God must have made me black because he wanted me to prove something. I was so proud of my discovery that I ran downstairs to tell my mother.

I remember saying, " I just figured out why I was born black. 'Cause if I'd been born white, than everything would be so easy and I wouldn't be so special."

My mother gave me a look that said. "Yeah, you're special all right. Specially weird!"

Of course she didn't say anything like that.

She probably said something like, "That's nice. Now go take a nap."

Because I was usually such a shy, quiet child (my actual nickname was Shy), whenever I put together more than a few sentences, my mother assumed I was overtired.

I didn't care. I had just figured out how I could reframe my racial shame. I convinced myself that it wasn't that I didn't want to be black; I was just going to be black in a completely different way—different than those people on the news. I decided that I was put on this earth to single-handedly show the world that black people were not all the same, that we could be special. The only way I knew to prove how special I could be as a black girl was to do everything white girls did and do it just as well or better. I think from that moment on, it became my mission. I wasn't running from being black; I was running toward being a different kind of black.

It kind of worked. In Catholic grade school, I hung with the Irish Catholic crowd that was nice and smart, but not so popular 'cause they didn't have as much money and weren't as blond. I was totally accepted there. Then the neighborhood "changed" and a lot of my Irish Catholic friends moved away; and the school started to get more African American students. That was a strange period because the black students didn't know what to do with me and vice versa. So I became best friends with the one Puerto Rican girl in the school and together we were able to straddle both the black and the white worlds. But I still ran away from being too black. No afro for me. No loosening up of the way I spoke. And no promiscuity! No way was I going to have the Stinkin' Shame Chorus sung about me!

The first year of high school was a challenge. I was going to an academically specialized all girls public school. It seemed like the perfect environment to continue being the Super Special Black Girl. But I quickly discovered that even though I was one of a handful of black girls in my class, the other black girls were smart and special, too. The first semester I attached myself to the siblings of my sister's friends who were a whole different kind of black: the Lightbrights. Lightbrights were an unequivocally special breed of blacks for two reasons: They were light-skinned (hence the name) and they had money. I was on the borderline of both those criteria. Being around lightbrights brought out a whole other type of shame! I was suddenly ashamed not only of being black but of being too black for the extra-special blacks. I did not know how to reframe that. I needed another tribe. I discovered theater.

I heard an announcement over the loudspeaker in homeroom class for an afterschool play audition at the boys' school down the street. I realized this could solve two of my problems. I could get relief from the crippling shyness I still struggled with *and* make a new group of friends. It worked on both counts. In Drama Club, we fancied ourselves "hippies" (even though that era was already dead), loving and accepting each other was our mission. But it was through Drama Club that I experienced my first two real encounters with racism.

The first incident happened in the middle of the first show I was cast in. There was a kiss. The male lead, Oedipus, had to kiss me, the Sphinx. A few weeks before the show, the actor playing Oedipus dropped out. He was pressured by his parents; they didn't want him kissing a black girl. Honestly, I have been in such denial about this incident that I had buried this memory for over thirty years. Only writing this essay brought it back to my consciousness. The second experience is very fitting to tell here in the Shame Prom 'cause it's part of the reason the Shame Prom is the only prom I'll ever attend.

I didn't attend either of my proms partly because it wasn't cool back in my day (hippies and proms didn't mix), but mostly because being at an all-girls school meant you had to find someone to ask and . . . come on, my shyness didn't completely disappear. However, I was asked to a prom at our brother school by a dear friend of mine from Drama Club. It was going to be a blast. The friend who asked me was a great guy who happened to be deaf. He could read lips really well and speak in that way that deaf people learn to speak. The interesting thing was that both of his parents were deaf, too. You can imagine the biases and problems they had to endure, right? However, when they found out that their son was taking a girl who wasn't Jewish to the prom, they forbade it.

It's interesting that I wasn't furious after each of these incidents. But I wasn't. Hurt, yes. Ashamed? Definitely. But not angry. Why? Because

I understood those parents. On some level I had been trained to empathize with them. They had no way of knowing I was a Super Special Black Girl. To them, I was just like all those people on the evening news. I knew what it was like to judge black people harshly because I did it myself. Instead of making me angry, these incidents added to my feelings of shame and my desire to prove something.

In college, my racial shame had other repercussions. I was a theater major, living on campus at a predominately white Long Island private college. Freshmen year, I was the only person of color in my class and one of two in the whole department. But that didn't bother me. By now, I was used to it. I preferred it. There was no pressure to really fit it. I couldn't totally ever fit in. I was black! And I got to use all of my Super Special Black Girl powers. I could be smart, funny, polite, charming, responsible, and special. All those things that weren't shown in the media. It was college, so Caucasian boys could date me without parental interference.

However, the black students on campus didn't appreciate my Super Special Black Girl powers. They taunted my roommate and me, wrote things on our door, and one evening we came home to find a pile of feces in front of our dorm room. That brought out two kinds of racial shame—the shame that black people would actually do that and the shame of not being black enough. This shame was different from the being-too-black shame I had felt with the Lightbrights and different from the I'm-embarrassed-to-be-black shame I felt when I watched the news or saw the shit at my door. This not-black-enough shame sometimes made me wonder if the great discovery I had as an eight-year-old might be flawed. My references, my experiences, my speech, my tastes were just not black enough for a lot of black people and that caused me shame whenever I was around them.

Fast forward to 2008, when I walked into my first phone-bank experience for Barack Obama. I was totally used to being the only or one of the few people of color in a room, but this time it was different. The sight of a majority of white volunteers passionately devoting their weekend to making phone calls for a black presidential candidate filled me with pride. I don't remember if I had ever let myself feel proud to be black before. I also felt relief. For the first time, I felt I could walk into a situation as a minority and not have to wear my Super Special Black Girl cape. Finally I felt like I no longer had to single-handedly prove that one could be both black and special. Now there was another very visible super special black person and he was all over the news! That's when I let myself realize how much shame I had been carrying and how maybe it was time to let some of it go.

It wasn't just the fact that white people were admiring and celebrating an African American—this had happened before. And it wasn't just that we elected a black president. What really ended my shame game (and I think my mother's, too, I might add) was watching Obama himself. Watching him humbly and graciously embrace victory; watching him weather accusations, mistakes, name-calling, resistance, hatred, and failures and still refuse to play the race card; watching him keep his dignity and his beliefs and his integrity and his comfort in himself; watching him soldier through all of this because he believes he has something that he wants to accomplish, something that he wants to contribute. He refuses to let the color of his skin get in the way of that. He has shown me by example something that I committed myself to at eight years old but never really truly believed was possible. Now I know that it is.

My son will soon graduate from Yale University. He's biracial, but there's no denying he's a person of color. He was born in a completely different era than I, but I wonder how different his experience was. My grandmother was no longer alive to lead the Stinkin' Shame Chorus, but the tune was expertly preserved and passed down. It was sung by my mother/his grandmother and my aunts and uncles, by my sister, and I'm sure I've sung a few verses myself. And because my son was academically gifted and raised in affluent downtown Manhattan, he was and still is almost always one of the few or only persons of color in his classes and other social situations. Does he feel the same need to don a Super Special Black Boy cape? I think he does. Does he feel the same amount of shame as I did? I'm sure he doesn't. Because some things *have* changed; now if we watch the evening news, there are people of color delivering it; there are still people of color doing bad things but there are people of color doing really good things. And of course, the biggest change of all is there is a person of color in the White House.

※

Yes, we will always be judged by the color of our skin. I accepted that a long time ago. But now I do not always feel that that judgment intrinsically implies that I am dangerous, lazy, stupid, unattractive, and powerless. I hope my son feels the same way. There will always be people who look at us and make negative assumptions. But thank God, *I* won't be one of them.

Am I completely shame-free? Not at all. I still feel a tightening in my chest when I watch or read the news. I'm feeling shame now as I complete this essay. I fear people will judge my acknowledgment of my shame, which will cause me more shame.

Then I think about the many family members who did not live to see our first black president. Many members of the Stinkin' Shame choir were taken far too early—succumbing to cancer, a disease associated with the suppression of emotions. I can't help but wonder if it was shame that killed them. I believe looking shame in the face, naming it, calling it out, and kicking it in the butt has health benefits, mentally and physically. It's scary and it's risky, and I'm worried that I've revealed too much, but I'm glad to have had the opportunity.

WHAT *Robyn* HOPES READERS WILL TAKE AWAY FROM HER STORY

"I would like people to get real: None of us is color-blind. It's a neurological and psychological impossibility. Race always matters, as do sex, attractiveness, height, weight, status, money, etc. These things may matter on different levels to different people but they matter. Getting real with how it matters to you and how it impacts your thinking and judgments is nothing to be ashamed of and is important for forming authentic relationships with others and with yourself."

ORIGINAL BRA
Meredith Resnick

⋮

I get my first bra when I am thirteen, even though I think of what I have as a chest, not breasts. I don't want a bra, whether I need one or not. But I soon find out that doesn't matter.

My new breasts attract attention. Breasts in general are a topic of conversation for girls and boys. Girls talk about busts and bras and curves and exercises that make tiny endowments swell to prize proportions. Boys talk about laying hands on endowments—the bigger, the better. I eavesdrop on these conversations, linger on the outskirts. I'm curious but I do not wear a bra and do not acknowledge I need one, so I have no right to talk. That is fine with me.

My aunt, my mother's sister, wants me to discuss my breasts and how they grow month by month, but she does all the talking. She thinks this will help me get over my shyness about my breasts. But I'm not shy; I'm private. Especially when she points at my breasts like they're ripe tomatoes ready for picking and declares, "Look at how you're blooming; you're a real bloomer!"

It doesn't help when she lifts her hands, palms up in front of her like she's hefting two bowling balls, and waddles around in circles sing-songing every word she knows for breasts. But she does it anyway.

The hardest part is when she takes my mother by the elbow and sighs, "Your baby is growing bosoms; you will have to take her brassiere shopping soon."

My mother grows tense. My aunt grins and stares. If I leave the room, they know I am upset and will talk about me behind my back. That is the worst.

The best I can do is slouch my shoulders forward and cross my arms. Without missing a beat, my mother tells me to stop hiding myself and stand up straight. She has told me this before. But when I comply, I feel her eyes on me, as though she is looking at a stranger. I want to hide.

I hate the word brassiere. It is a grown-up word; it sounds sexy and sexy is grown up. Sometimes I feel sexy and it scares me because I feel like someone else. I feel something I don't understand well up inside me. But then I look in the mirror at my skinny arms and long neck. Sexy is beautiful. I'm not.

My mother has a love-hate relationship with beauty. She describes her own body in a way that is at once conceited and repulsed. "I have gorgeous calves," she says, posing as a model would for Chanel, or pointing her toe like a drum majorette. She peeks in the full-length mirror, lifting her chin ever so slightly, then wilts. "Too bad my thighs look like meat loaves." Calves: good; thighs: bad. All I know is that when she ends up laughing about it, so do I.

She talks incessantly about her rear end, which she's dubbed the Gordon ass, a term I hate because our last name is Gordon. This means I, by default, have such an ass—a bit large and round, but, according to her, not in the flattering way. The kind of ass that makes a statement, the statement being that my mother hates it and, ipso facto, so must I.

She has something to say about her stomach and the appendix scar, a long dimpled line across her belly that looks like someone has taken a knife and sliced through raw bread dough. She hates it. She likes her blue eyes and her high, sharp cheekbones but bemoans her stick-straight red hair and skimpy eyelashes. She wants my hair—dark, coarse, ringed like a DNA helix—but that is my father's genetic gift, not hers. She loves her smile but hates her teeth—Berkowitz buckers, she calls her caps, after the dentist who "installed" them. Her lips are too full, yet her nose is regal, as is her chin, which she loves, because it helps hide her fleshy neck. On the bright side, her freckles are an asset simply because she likes them.

She talks of almost everything, except her breasts, and her brassieres—the few she owns that she slips on in the dark, that lay in her drawer, pushed far back. Her bras do not dry on the shower rod and she does not own a black bra. She rarely buys new ones because she says she doesn't like to try them on. The outline through the back of her shirt is the only clue that she wears a bra, or owns one.

My father, on the other hand, wears his boxers and undershirts around the house. He calls her shy, modest, and, sometimes, a prude, which is a word I do not understand, and must look up in the dictionary. The dictionary definition—a person who is excessively proper or modest in speech, conduct, dress—lacks the disdain I hear in my father's voice when he says it. She pretends she doesn't hear him. But there is something else.

My father also has the habit of commenting on all the pretty women who walk by and, as a child, I thought when she talked about my father's wandering eye she meant an eye that went for a stroll. My mother had begun seeing a psychiatrist, a man, to whom she complained about my father. He told my mother she should point out to her husband all the pretty ladies, the ones she'd think he'd find attractive before he could point them out to her. She explained the idea was of the head-'em-off-at-the-pass variety, the I-saw-it-first genre. If my mother could identify the ladies my father might like and say them aloud first, including what was pretty about them and how she might want the same attributes, she would avoid the humiliation of being caught off-guard.

But now the problem is me, not the ladies on the street whom my mother thinks are prettier than she is. I fight to change her mind but end up crying. Her words hurt. Sometimes I think she doesn't want me to grow up. Like when I wear pantyhose with my dresses instead of knee socks. When I don't wear my hair in two long braids anymore, or forget to wear a robe with my nightgown. Like the times when my father looks at me like I am not a little girl anymore and my mother sees him looking. I am still his little girl, but I am less little and girl now. I am thirteen, a young lady, and I am sensitive, not only to the words boys my age say about a girl's breasts, but about what I imagine men my father's age might say, and not always with actual words, but with a turn of the head, a stare held a moment too long.

If she could keep me a girl, keep me someone who fathers and brothers and boys don't look at, maybe that will make her happy. If I don't wear a bra, I defy my body. I want to make my body agree with what I think she wants. At thirteen, I think she wants this because she never suggests we go bra shopping.

Instead my mother and I argue, and I cry. My father is the one who soothes my hurt with a gentle voice, a funny joke. My mother sometimes gets mad when he does this. She never used to, but now she feels like we are against her. My father's words were always a neutral area; now they are a war zone. I wish I could talk to my mother about it, but she turns my words against me. My emotions upset her. Emotion upsets her.

※

The girls in fourth-period P.E. don't understand why I don't wear a bra.

They say something like, "Does the word *bra* mean anything to you?"

They say flat-out, "Girls who attend Foothills Junior High School in Arcadia, California, wear bras."

They tell me because I just moved from New York. They think in New York everyone burned their bras so no one wears any.

The girls say, "We saw your upstairs private parts because you don't wear a bra."

They were behind me during squat thrusts and push-ups and could see up my gym shirt when it billowed away from my body. The girls pat me on the back and assure me they weren't trying to look, that they tried hard not to look, and that even though they saw it all, they weren't staring. Then one of them giggles.

Didn't your mother take you bra shopping when you started junior high? they question. I shake my head because I cannot make words come out of my mouth.

One of the girls wags a finger at me and says, "Well tell your mother we all have the same bras and you get them at JCPenney."

The five nod in approval. One unsnaps her gym blouse as we shuffle back to the locker room. She faces me, holds her white blouse open with her fingertips, turns her torso left then right like a model so I see all angles of the JC Penney bra. It is dainty like a lace doily and white like milk. The cups are filled with something that makes her tiny breasts look like two golf balls stuck to her chest. The bra has a teensy pink rosette on the bodice and, she points out, the bra straps adjust.

The word *bra* sounds better to me than *brassiere* does. I watch her snap up her blouse and say, "But do I really need one?"

"Everyone needs one in junior high!" they chime. It doesn't matter what you look like. They tell me it's not about how big I am, it's about what grade I'm in. We're not kids, they say. We all wear them and if you don't, the boys think you're easy.

One adds, "That's the only reason the boys talk to you."

I feel naked and stupid and cannot hide anymore. What I've tried to keep secret is no secret. I hope the boys across the blacktop can't see through my shirt. I cross my arms, curl my shoulders, and go to my locker. I put my street clothes back on. I wear a sweater over my blouse the rest of the day. Even though it is eighty-five degrees outside, I button it.

＊

Later I tell my mother the bra story. She braces herself against the white Formica countertop in my sister's kitchen, where we are staying since we moved from New York. My mother's face is the color of snow. It makes her nervous, this bra talk. My aunt should be here to tell her it's brassiere shopping time.

All my mother says is, "You never wanted a bra before; you never asked."

For the first time I wonder why she never asked me, told me, that I needed one. Her voice sounds blaming, but I shed no tears. It doesn't matter. I have to get a bra. I can't help the way I look or that I am looked at. Still, she does not say when we will go bra shopping.

My older sister wants to help but she doesn't take me bra shopping; that is something a mother does. My sister could be my mother; she is twenty-one years older than I am. She tells me that she doesn't remember our mother taking her bra shopping either, and she seems at once annoyed and resigned that the chore to outfit me in my first bra has fallen to her.

My sister stands by the window in her dressing room and the warm autumn winds pull the sheer curtains flat against the open frame. She extends her hand and in it, bunched up in a wad no bigger than a plum is my first bra. The straps are scrambled between her fingers and the fine mesh cups rest in her palm.

Here, wear this, she says. I don't wear it anymore.

She lets the bra slip from her hand. One strap loops around her index finger and the bra dangles in midair. Here, try it, she says extending her arm.

This is my first bra. It is the color of sand. Playground sand from a sandbox. A yellow brown. Next to my skin it looks the color of uncooked oatmeal. Pasty. Its tiny cups are frayed and snags dot the material. It is soft.

I go to my bedroom and close the door. I sit cross-legged on the bed and place my first bra in front of me. I stick my gym socks in the cups to see how it looks filled up. I decide not to try the bra on, but know the time has come to wear it, even if it isn't from JCPenney.

I think only of the girls in fourth-period P.E. with their crisp white bras with tiny rosettes, with fuzzy layers of padding that fill space where nothing else does. My bra has no filling, no roses, and it is see-through. It had been used and it looks like something a woman wears, not a thirteen-year-old. But I will wear it anyway.

My mother stays out of my room and doesn't ask about my new bra. She doesn't ask if I want to go bra shopping because why shop? I have a bra now. If I want to buy a bra, I will have to go myself.

Years later I will shop for my own bras. Sometimes I will stand in the dressing room with the distinct feeling I am doing something wrong because I am doing something that acknowledges my femininity. I will overcome my shyness and buy bras meant to be removed by men; I will look for the laciest, most seductive, prettiest piece of lingerie I can find, then buy two. I will practice looking at myself, examining my body, then getting dressed because I've read this will help me be more comfortable with myself. And I will learn, through the sheer practice of standing up straight in hundreds of dressing rooms before even more full-length mirrors, that all the confused feelings I felt at thirteen—wanting to hide myself yet be acknowledged—still live in me, that it's normal. That for my mother, it never felt normal.

☀

I will know all this because I will not be that little girl anymore.

WHAT *Meredith* HOPES READERS WILL TAKE AWAY FROM HER STORY

"I hope readers will be inspired to write, draw, paint, sing, diagram, or in some way document their own story."

WHAT I KNOW OF SILENCE
Brooke Elise Axtell

⋮

My mom is in the hospital. The doctors say she will never walk again. She can't speak, so she writes notes to me. "I love you," she says. "I love you," I write back. "You don't have to write. You can talk," she writes slowly on the scrap of paper.

But I want to write. I do not want to speak if she cannot speak. This is her language, the written word, and I want to live where she lives, so she does not feel alone. I am the child, but she looks like the child, a pale doll in her white gown surrounded by tubes. I don't know what to say, so I bring her a poem about a lamb who cannot find her flock. She encourages me to read my poem aloud. I begin to speak.

My brothers laugh when I reach the part about the loneliness, so I crawl under a table and hide while the nurse comes in to tend to my mom. "How are you?" the nurse asks warmly. "I read a poem," I reply, as if that explains everything. What I do not say is this: I am afraid. I am afraid I am going to lose her. I am afraid that she will stay like this, a pale doll, and never come back to life.

Since my mom was unable to care for us at this time and my father had to travel often for his work, my parents hired nannies. One after another. The fat Irish ladies who smoked cigarettes and left us in the house alone, telling us that it was "hide and go seek." The woman from India who stole my mom's credit card and showed us movies about strippers. The sensitive Polish woman whose husband painted landscapes with prize horses. The baton twirler from Iowa. The two women from Ethiopia who smiled often and made rich, spicy food. The woman, Dee Dee, who had thick blond hair falling down to her lower back and later married a man named Dee. The woman with the wiry hair, mouse-face, and glasses who wrapped a towel around me when I got out of the tub. I loved the African ladies the most. One of them slept in my room for a while. She smelled like red spices and shea butter body cream.

Then there was Jim.

Jim with his baseball caps and plaid shirts.

Jim, who played video games and refused to wash the dishes.

Jim, who went to seminary and raped me.

Jim, who told me that it was God's will because "everything that happens is God's will."

Jim, who said that I was evil and made him do this to me, entering my body as he prayed, "Our Father. . . ."

"God is punishing you for your sins. If you tell anyone, I will kill you and then I will kill your family."

I believed Jim. I was already desperately afraid of losing my mom. I retreated deeper into silence and did not tell anyone what happened to me. I felt dirty and disgusting, that somehow I deserved this.

Jim tied me up and called me a whore. He gave me to other men who pay to rape little girls and film it for their private pornography collections. One day, he took me into the basement of a large home where there was a cot, some chains, a camera, and a cage. In between rounds of abuse, they would put me in the cage and laugh at me, calling me a cunt. I did not even know what that meant, but I knew it must be the most worthless thing on earth.

I don't know how long I was there. It felt like days, but they may have drugged me. There were other children being abused and filmed. Their faces still haunt me. I am not going to tell you everything they did to us because I have said enough for you to know where I have been.

But I will tell you this: Through the creativity of my mind and the fierce love in my heart, I survived.

I imagined myself floating up out of my body through the lens of the camera into another world, a place of refuge. In my refuge, there was a crystal stream and a white horse. No one could touch me there. I imagined that my abuse was just a film inside my mind and stored it away until the day I was ready to look at it again.

My parents had no reason to believe I had been abused. I was focused in school and expressive at home, and any signs of distress could easily be attributed to my mom's illness and the constant parade of nannies. I was a peaceful, bright, compassionate child.

I tucked my film away along with the shame and tried to please my parents as much as I could.

There were minor incidents of acting out that could have provoked their curiosity, but I was careful to hide the evidence. I started to steal from my friends. In second grade, I was caught stealing a silver ring with a tiny shell that a girl took off during gym class. When she told our teacher it was missing, Miss Elko asked all of us to empty our pockets. I emptied mine and did not even try to conceal my treasure. I studied Elko's fake hot pink nails and frosted blond hair, sprayed high above her head, and lied.

"These aren't my clothes," I said. "I stayed at a friend's house last night and she let me borrow her clothes. I don't know how it got there." I returned the ring to my classmate. My face was burning, but I never confessed. I felt justified because it was beautiful and I wanted it even if I never wore it because I was so hungry for beauty. Besides, the girl was mean and had a pig face. She also had a habit of pulling my hair. After my experience with Jim, I could not tolerate a bully.

When I rode my bike around the neighborhood, proud of the purple seat and handle bars, I never stopped to talk with other kids. One day, a handsome boy with pale blond hair and blue eyes called out to me. "Do you want to help me paint my skateboard?"

I was stunned and lost my breath. I wanted more than anything else to stop and join him. He was my secret crush from class and I was thrilled that he noticed me. My whole body flooded with joy. I began to approach him and then stopped. Desire quickly turned to fear. I thought, "If I stay here, I might get hurt. He might want to have sex with me. If I get hurt, it will be my fault." So, I turned away saying, "I need to get home." He never tried to talk to me again.

There was another boy in the second grade who passed a note to me in class. I was so excited to open it. It said:

Dear Brooke,
Do you want to come over to my house
and watch T.V. and have sex with me?

Below that he drew a picture of a T.V. I was frightened that someone else wanted to have sex with me and he confirmed my fear that it wasn't just older men who would hurt me, but boys, too. I showed the note to my Mom, but didn't tell her about Jim and how sick I felt inside. She was concerned and tried to reach my teacher, but my teacher said it never happened and that I had lied. When I discovered that my teacher would not even believe that a boy in my class asked to have sex with me, I knew that I could never tell anyone about what happened with Jim.

Soon after this, I became friends with Stephanie, my next-door neighbor who was in eighth grade at the time. Her birth parents abused her, and for years she would not speak. Eventually the family next door adopted her. Her mother was kind and gave me milk with cookies. Her older brother traveled and came back with a piece of the Berlin Wall. Stephanie taught me how to play games, how to "kiss" her vagina. She never physically forced me. She did not have to. I was seven and I understood that this was expected of me. Once again, I did not speak about my experience to anyone. I forced the shame underground and pretended it never happened.

I was raised in a fundamentalist Christian Church where I was taught that I must remain a virgin until marriage in order to please God. This was very confusing since Jim told me that everything that happened to me was God's will. I wondered if it was God's will for me to be abused and if so, how could he expect me to be a virgin? It all seemed unfair. I was also taught that homosexuality is evil, so I knew that I could never tell anyone about Stephanie. Growing up, I danced in a professional ballet company with gay men and I could not comprehend how they could be evil. They were exuberant, creative, and kind. They were the way men *should* be. They made me feel beautiful when I was so hungry for beauty.

I turned to poetry as a child because it was the only way I could speak the unspeakable. It is the language of invention and possibility. I wanted above all else to bring a new world into being, but until that day arrived, I devoted myself to writing in my turquoise journal, carefully crafting the codes and symbols to hold my secrets.

As a girl, I transmuted grief into poems filled with images of suffering animals and the mystical joys of nature. I wrote about the roots of an old oak tree that mysteriously cleared away my troubles. In junior high, I wrote about addicts and prostitutes, the outcasts and the mentally ill. I kept circling the seed of what I had seen, what I was forbidden to see.

As a woman, I visited my parents' home and looked through a box of art I created in grade school. I sifted through pictures of rainbows, aliens, haunted houses, and my attempt at drawing Jesus. At the bottom of the box, I found a little blue lamb who was crying. On the back, in black ink, it said, "All we like sheep have gone astray."

For many years, I hated my body because my body refused to forget. I could not stand to be in front of a camera or have my picture taken because I felt like I was being captured all over again. Sometimes, I would wonder if they still had the pictures, if they were still getting off on my pain.

Each day, I woke up wanting to die. Every small task was a struggle. I still had not told anyone about what happened as a child. My silence was slowly killing me.

I turned to drinking—tequila—to calm and enliven me. I wanted my voice to be heard, to carry a message of healing power, but I still felt conflicted about being seen. When I had to go to a photo shoot for my music career, I would suddenly feel vulnerable.

I sang at night and slept most of the afternoon, often into the evening. One night, I heard a pounding on my window. The A&R rep from RCA was at the club in Austin to see me perform and the show started in fifteen minutes. I threw on a long black skirt and black camisole and headed over to meet the band. I entered the stage as the drums came in and fell into a hypnotic state, my nightly dervish. I opened my mouth and felt the soul of the earth sing through me.

After the show, the rep took me out to dinner. He said, "Your voice sounds like Fiona Apple, but your performance style is more like Tori Amos. Do you know Paula Cole? I signed her. I can't sign you now, but someone will by the end of the year."

I was relieved. As much as I wanted to share my words through music, I still did not know if I wanted to be visible. I struggled for years with suicidal thoughts and the sense that this world would be a better place without me. I constantly distanced myself from those who loved me most because I felt toxic, cursed, as if I would somehow attract evil into their lives. I hid in my studio and stopped returning phone calls for weeks at a time.

I ended up working with incredible musicians: Charlie Sexton (who toured with Bob Dylan), Stephen Bruton (who toured with Bonnie Raitt), and Mitch Watkins (who toured with Leonard Cohen and Lyle Lovett). I recorded a couple of CDs and heard my songs on the radio, but I felt like a fraud. I told my manager that I didn't feel like a singer. He laughed.

"Well, you're going to have to get over that," he said warmly.

One of his other acts, Los Lonely Boys, as gaining momentum, so even more opportunities were opening up for me. He came into the studio one day during a recording session and said that the head of Sony had listened to my latest demo and loved my voice. I felt as though he was talking about someone else.

❄

Eventually I decided to go underground in search of a healing path. I left the music world behind and moved to Boulder, Colorado, to study poetry and Buddhist meditation at Naropa University. I started attending a recovery group for survivors of childhood sexual abuse and began to recognize how the beliefs I formed as a little girl colored everything I touched.

Before I felt compassion for myself, I felt fierce compassion for the other women in my group. To learn how to value myself, I imagined what I would want for them and then chose to embrace that vision. When they talked about how they had been used and exploited, how they still struggled to feel any sense of worth, I knew I was willing to do whatever I could to contribute to their healing. With their help, I created a body of knowledge, a body that finally belongs to me.

In my meditation class, I learned about aspirations as a contemplative practice, a way to offer loving kindness to ourselves and the world. Whenever I had flashbacks, I would turn to my own aspiration as a touchstone, a way to ground myself in the present moment: "May all who have suffered as I have suffered be liberated from their suffering and the roots of their suffering. May they be guided even now to what they need for complete liberation and healing." I turned to this mantra to remind myself that I am not alone and that through my own recovery I can bring hope to many.

Isolation is an illusion. So many of us have suffered through violence against our bodies, souls, and minds. I hope that by sharing my story and what I've learned through recovery, women will be inspired to break open their silences. Suffering can be the seed of awakening. When we awaken, we encourage others to do the same.

Sexual assault sends the message that our voices and our desires do not matter. Creative expression provides a sacred space for honoring the truth of our experience so we can begin to heal. In the midst of my pain, I sensed that if could draw pictures of the abuse, write about the abuse, and bring every trace of shame into the light, it could not destroy me. No matter what happened, I could bear witness and embrace myself with tenderness.

This is what I went underground to find: the root of the root, the core of my need, a defiant love that would not let me go. Step by step, I have reconnected with my power and worth. I have forged the path of a radical recovery: the transformative power of inner healing that gives birth to social justice. In my work as an advocate for survivors of gender violence, I have the opportunity to help women reclaim their creative gifts. Through their poetry, music, visual art, films, and jewelry, I see their resilience and dignity. I know a woman is healing when she starts to value her voice—as I now value my own.

WHAT *Brooke* HOPES READERS WILL TAKE AWAY FROM HER STORY

"In our deepest shame, we are all just children hungry for love. The hunger is wise. Let it lead you home."

THE HAIR MANIFESTO
Marianne Schnall

:

There are so many sagas I could tell you about my hair. I could probably fill a whole book and call it *The Hair Monologues*. Suffice to say that my relationship with my hair has been a huge factor in my life.

It started with the basic premise, around thirteen, that I simply had the wrong hair. My hair was naturally curly and brown. Barbie's hair was blond and straight. All of the models featured in the magazines had straight hair, and almost every issue offered advice on how curly-haired girls could straighten theirs. Almost all of my friends had straight hair, too. Their hair was neat, smooth, and shiny, and always could be counted on to look the same. My hair was wild, dull, shapeless, and vulnerable to environmental factors, like humidity or rain, which could, without warning, cause my hair to frizz up within seconds of impact. It was, so it seemed, stressful hair to have.

So, I began blow-drying it. It required quite a bit of time, at least twenty minutes every day. It would sometimes get so hot in my bathroom that I would often move my whole blow-drying operation in front of the air conditioner, sitting on the floor peering into a compact mirror.

And then there was the weather-related stress. During high school, at the height of social pressures, and just when I began dating boys, if I had plans to go out, I would religiously check the weather hotline in the days prior to the event and often hourly on the day of. Anything over about 75 percent humidity, or, even worse, rain, meant my night was ruined. My hair would frizz—the gig would be up. All of my hard blow-drying work would be zapped within seconds into one giant frizz ball, much like Cinderella poofed back into rags at the ball, and I would be revealed as the straight-hair imposter I was. Back then, and I kid you not, the weather had an enormous impact on my psyche and well-being—it would be funny, if it weren't so tragic. I can actually remember several instances when I made up an excuse and canceled plans because it was just too humid for my hair and me to venture out.

❄

I can remember many times going to the Caribbean with my family, and how in the relentless heat and humidity, my hair was destined to be a curly frizz ball at all times. I would try vainly to slick it back in a ponytail so my curly hair wouldn't be so obvious, or even give off the impression that it would be straight if I just let it down. I always felt so ugly when my hair wasn't its low-humidity, straight-pretending self.

And then there were the products. I tried them all. Every new straightening shampoo, gel, mousse, conditioner—if it said it helped straighten hair, I had to buy it. I was on a romantic quest to find the perfect product—the magic tonic that would finally transform me. Hundreds, if not thousands, of my consumer dollars went toward hair products.

In tenth grade, my friend Amy and I decided to dye our hair with some over-the-counter Clairol product. I would have to describe the color as "banana" blond. From then on, I was Barbie with straight, blond hair. But unlike Barbie, mine required a lot of work.

It was around this time that for no apparent reason, I decided to call myself Chris. I had always hated my name—Marianne—it sounded so uncool, so dorky, and reminded everyone of Maryanne on Gilligan's Island. Don't ask me why I chose Chris—perhaps it had something to do with Cheryl Ladd's character on *Charlie's Angels,* and I guess it sounded to me like the hip girl with straight blond hair I was desperately trying to become. I had everybody at my school calling me Chris for years. My parents weren't too thrilled about this as you might imagine. I eventually gave it up, but my name change is immortalized in one of my high school yearbooks in a caption under my picture where I am called Chris Schnall. I had been victorious in convincing everybody, including myself, that I was someone else.

Unfortunately, I also developed various manifestations of eating disorders (in high school one of my best friends was anorexic, another bulimic), which I have only recently overcome. I can think of so many examples of abuse I put my body through—all because I simply refused to accept my body the way it was. Aside from the years I fried my hair with a blow-dryer, I spent many years sun-tanning for the dark skin I thought looked better (which elevated my risk of skin cancer), and decades dieting to achieve a body that was possible only for supermodels.

But, of course, back to my hair. All that blow-drying continued right through college and beyond, until I was thirty years old. That's about seventeen years of blow-drying time. I calculated it at a half-hour a day for seventeen years, and it came to approximately 2,856 hours of my life.

My hair awakening started when I became pregnant with my first child. The first shift came when I decided to stop dyeing my hair blond, because even though my hairdresser swore it was safe, my new maternal instinct just didn't like the thought of dousing my head with toxic, smelly chemicals when I was growing a baby inside me. Growing my hair out and gaining weight while pregnant was my first body revolution. I had an excuse for not looking my best since I was pregnant. I was actually happy to get back to my own light-brown color. For the first time in my life, everyone was telling me how much I looked like my mother.

Once my baby was born, it was harder and harder to find the time or energy to blow-dry my hair, to keep up the charade, which suddenly didn't seem so important. So I just stopped. Cold turkey. It was freeing. I gained a half hour a day, a welcome development in the chaos of life with a newborn baby. However, I still didn't like my hair, and thus began another raid at the drugstore of every curly-hair product. Now my goal was to have shiny, springy, frizzless ringlets à la Nicole Kidman (when she wasn't straightening hers). I was the hair product industry's best customer. My graveyard of hair products could fill up a whole room.

What happened since has been a subtle evolution, but I have grown to accept and even love my hair. I have found the perfect hair products, the Alterna line, which happens to be made from hempseed. I must be fully stocked at all times. This doesn't mean that I always think my hair looks great. It has its good and bad days, but thank god I don't have my whole well-being wrapped around it anymore. Rainy or humid weather doesn't even faze me. Sure, my hair might get a little frizzy, but we'll all live through it.

Today, I have two beautiful daughters. My five-year-old has wavy brown hair and my two-year old has straight blond hair—go figure. Yes, I gave in to the Barbie dolls. In fact, my older daughter has lots of them, but she has lots of other types of dolls, too, so they are just part of the population. She gets into very creative, imaginative play with her dolls, which appears healthy enough at this point. But you can be sure I am on alert, on the lookout, for any emerging hair neurosis. And I will also be on the lookout for eating disorders.

What this represents is about so much more than hair—it is about self-acceptance. How unfortunate that we women spend so much time and energy fixated on how we look. Many of us have stepped over the line from wanting to look good to downright obsession. So much of my struggle, my unhappiness, my fear seems to be rooted in this refusal to accept myself for who I am. Trying to reconnect with myself now is like going on an archaeological dig to someplace completely new and uncharted. I must dig really deep and peer through the dark, cobwebbed corners of myself to find my true essence, discover my true nature. What I am working on grooming now, on making smooth and shiny, is on my inside. Hokey, but true. My hair isn't such a big part of my story anymore. It is now just that—my hair.

This past summer, I had promised my older daughter that on my birthday I would jump off the diving board at the pool, something my hair concerns had prevented me from ever doing before. I did a "pencil"—just jumped straight down with my arms closely at my sides. It was like a slow-motion baptism, sinking down into the cold, clear water. It felt wonderful, and symbolized a sort of rebirth. An hour or so later, while we were still at the pool, much of the East Coast lost power—I hoped my hair cataclysm didn't have anything to do with it.

The moral of the story, if any good or wisdom can be gleaned from this hair opera, is the lesson contained in those 2,856 wasted hours of my life, which doesn't take into account all the time spent calling the weather, worrying about my hair, and buying hair products. I am just now trying to shake off the shackles and pressures I've faced as a woman, to be something I am not. We are all born perfect beings. We don't need nose jobs, bigger boobs, differently colored or textured hair, Botoxed or sun-tanned skin. We don't need to spend so much time striving for the perfectly contoured body we will never have. That jewel inside us is all we need to polish, in order to truly be beautiful, be happy, and shine brightly.

I want to taste my own consciousness, find my own essence—not what I think others expect of me—but who I really am. I want to know myself, and aim to reach my own inner potential, my truth, my peace.

❄

I want to look in the mirror now and see me—and my hair—the way God created me, the divine artwork that I am.

WHAT *Marianne* HOPES READERS WILL TAKE AWAY FROM HER STORY

"That you will love and accept yourself—and not waste one precious second of your life striving to be something other than the amazing, unique individual you are."

SHAME NEVER WAS
Elizabeth Geitz

⋮

I was in the kitchen baking a bunny rabbit cake for my children when the call that forever changed my life came. I was in seminary studying to become an Episcopal priest and the schedule had been grueling. Spring break had finally arrived.

"Elizabeth, it's for you. It's your brother," my husband, Michael, called.

I hurried to the phone licking icing off my fingers.

"Elizabeth?" my brother said tentatively, his voice breaking.

"Brad, are you all right?"

"Mother killed herself this morning."

A scream. Where had it come from? It was an unearthly, eerie, guttural sound from the depths of something . . . despair, devastation, disbelief?

Michael rushed into the room. I dropped the phone. He grabbed it. "Brad, what is it?"

"Oh, no. Oh, no," he said, the color draining from his face.

I was a crumpled-up ball on the bed, unmoving, numb, my body shut down in self-protection. At least that's what Michael told me later. I have no memory of it to this day.

Within half an hour, I was sitting in the car in shock and denial telling my husband, "No, I'm fine. You come later. I know you have business meetings to attend."

What was I thinking? My life was falling apart. Had fallen apart and was spiraling downward quickly. But being the good wife or the good Southern woman that I was, take your pick—I said, "I'm fine. You go ahead, honey. I'll carry on. You can bring the children in a few days when I get everything sorted out."

Sorted out. Like I was going to sort out the laundry or straighten out a confused schedule. Right. No problem.

And I was on my way to my family home in Tennessee.

❄

As the plane began its descent into Nashville, I tried to remember the good times with my mother. I couldn't. She had threatened suicide since I was sixteen. When I finally had the courage to discuss it with my two brothers, I was surprised to learn that I was the only one who had lived with the fear of her threats and the overriding shame that went with it.

My mother wanted to kill herself. What did that say about me? I felt worthless. My life meant nothing if my own mother didn't love me enough to want to live.

So I set out to prove to her that I was worthy of love. I covered up the shame and the truth that I didn't matter enough. I made sure I mattered. Straight A's in high school. The right friends. The right college. The right job. If only I kept doing the right things, everything would work out. Everything would be fine and Mother would be happy.

But Mother wasn't happy.

And now she was dead.

In the morgue. When police arrived at our house that morning, they dusted my father's hands to make sure he hadn't shot her. Then they zipped my mother up in a black body bag and took her away.

When I arrived that afternoon, my parent's minister told me what the police had done to my father. "How dare they treat him like that?" I cried, filled with indignation. "How dare they? He'd just found his wife of forty-three years dead by her own hand! And they treat him like a criminal?" I was furious.

Several days later my mother's obituary appeared in the local newspaper, stating that she had died by self-inflicted gunshot wound. Still in shock, moving as if in a nightmare, I made it through the funeral and then back to my home in Princeton, New Jersey.

A year later, I was on the altar of the Episcopal Church that had sponsored me for ordination. The priest was holding up the chalice, reciting the words of Holy Communion. The blood of Christ and my mother's blood mingled in my mind, the association overwhelming me. I felt like I was going to faint. But I didn't. I kept going. And I kept doing the right things.

It was then that it hit me. Doing all the right things had not saved my mother and it was not going to save me. So I left for an eight-day silent retreat. I had to get away. I needed to be alone to think and pray.

On the third day I realized I was angry. No, not angry—enraged. All my life, I had done what I was supposed to do and what difference did it make?

In the silence of my well-lit room at the retreat center, containing only a single bed and an overstuffed recliner, I found myself screaming out loud over and over again. I felt a deep, searing pain that I wanted to somehow scream out of myself. "What difference does it make anyway?" I lamented aloud, hoping no one could hear me, not caring if they did.

I had come apart to be with the God who I believed had called me to become a priest, but I didn't want to be with a God who could let something like this happen. Each and every Sunday I had prayed to God, the Father Almighty. Never mind the problem of God as Father. In that moment I needed to deal with an Almighty God who was anything but.

So I did the worst thing I could think to do. I screamed at Jesus, "You're impotent! Impotent! How could you stand there and let her do this? She had a crucifix in her room. You were there. Right there when she put the gun in her mouth. Why didn't you stop her? Why? Because you're impotent. That's why. And I hate you. I hate you!"

And suddenly he was there. I hadn't felt God's presence in the year since my mother's suicide but there God was, in the form of Jesus. I couldn't see him; I felt him. Like you can feel someone looking at you before you turn around, with a sixth sense that defies explanation. And I was uncomfortable. I didn't want to feel Jesus' presence. He had failed me. He had let me down and left me with a searing shame that burned into me.

※

I had become the Queen of Shame. I hadn't told anyone in Princeton that my mother had killed herself. I covered up the truth. "Yes, it was sudden. No, it wasn't expected. Thank you, I'm fine." The "I'm fine" again. And I certainly didn't tell anyone what was behind it.

My father had declared bankruptcy ten years before. The next day my mother, who suffered from manic depression, had attempted suicide with pills and alcohol.

My parents called me that year on Christmas night. "Betsy, did you have a good Christmas?" they asked.

"Yes it was wonderful. Why?"

"We didn't want to ruin your Christmas, so we waited to call you after you'd finished opening your presents. Your father is filing bankruptcy and we're losing our home," my mother said, without missing a beat.

Silence. My normal reaction when confronted with devastating, earth-shattering news. I slowly died inside.

Our family home of twenty-eight years. Gone.

"Oh," I said. "Well . . . thanks for waiting to tell me." The next night my sister-in-law called from the emergency room. Mother had tried to kill herself. I told no one.

I was no stranger to shame and withholding the truth. My husband was a successful Wall Street investment banker and we were around people of success with a capital S all the time. I kept quiet to fit in, pretending to be like everyone else.

The longer I kept my secret in, the more powerful it became. When I went to visit my parents, they had moved to a completely different part of town. Losing face in a small Southern town can be devastating—and it was, to both of them and to me.

I felt shame when I went to visit. Shame when I drove their old car and guilty over my new one sitting in the garage at home. Shame that I couldn't just give them everything. Shame that I couldn't save them, save their lifestyle. Shame that our fall from grace was right there for everyone to see.

But it wasn't. I didn't live there. I lived in the very different world of Princeton—a world of family money, earned money, and Ivy League educations. I kept quiet, thinking, "If only they knew, they wouldn't like me. They'd know I don't really belong here. It's not just my accent that's different. It's me."

※

Ten years later, after my mother committed suicide, I was filled with a shame more insidious than the first. It was the shame deep in my soul that my mother had died by her own hand and I hadn't seen it coming. I felt the shame that I, a priest, was not there for her in her greatest hour of need and could not save her. I felt the shame of failure. Utter, abject failure.

Shame was my hidden, silent companion for many years. I dealt with it in therapy, spiritual direction, and with close friends. But, always in private, and so the shame remained. Unmovable.

Eventually keeping quiet and playing to an unseen, uncaring crowd that didn't exist became too costly. So I began to tell the truth about my family, my past, my mother, my failure to save her from herself. And in bringing the truth to light, I realized that my mother's depression was not about my failings or me. I had spent years trying to forgive my mother, but for me to be free, the person I really needed to forgive was myself. Finally, I was able to do that.

Gradually over a period of twenty years, the shame went away. I've learned that I am both more vulnerable and stronger because of my experience. I've learned that letting go of shame is one of the most free- ing things I've ever done. I've learned that I don't have to dance at the Shame Prom forever. The dress, the shoes, the long-wilted corsage are now gone. The music has finally stopped.

And with the learning and letting go has come remembering, rediscovering, recapturing. All the good times, the warm mother/daughter times before my mother's illness took control of her life. The homemade Southern bread and baked brownies waiting for me when I arrived home from school. Birthday parties. Shopping trips to Nashville. Late night talks about boys and who was dating whom. The countless tennis matches she drove me to during high school. Yes, she was the mother who was there, in spite of it all.

From the foundation of my faith tradition and a great deal of support, I found the strength to live as the wonderful child God created. It doesn't mean that the pain is gone. It will always be there no matter how often I deal with it. But it does mean that I can say yes, I am precious in God's sight. Somewhere the passage from Isaiah 43:4 sank in and I began to believe it with all my heart. Yes, I am precious. I matter. To God and to my family and to my friends and, yes, to myself. I matter enough to live my life differently than my mother was able to live hers.

What contributed to my mother's inability to grow into the fullness of the wonderful woman God created? Suicide is exceedingly complex, and my mother's manic depression was a significant factor. But what about societal factors? One profound influence in her life was the complicated role of religion. Although not necessarily a cause of her suicide, my mother's religious training did contribute to her depression, deep sense of shame, and lack of choices. She grew up in the '40s and '50s in the American Bible Belt, where there was a church on every corner. Where women were told they were created second and sinned first. Where women were told about God, the Father and Mother Mary, meek and mild, and about the many women in the Bible who didn't even have names.

The misuse and abuse of scripture leads women to believe they are second rate. Less than. Not as good as. It leads women to believe they don't matter, that God is male and therefore male is God.

Once I was able to accept myself, forgive myself, love myself, I knew I was meant to help other women love themselves. So I worked with women on welfare in the inner city where I learned that shame is the universal language. I wrote books about what the Bible really says about women and God and Jesus. It's not what you may have heard or been taught or left the church, synagogue, or mosque over. No. It's different. There are truths finally being written about today. A truth that is no longer hidden but out in the open. The truth that shame does not belong to you and to me, my sisters. No. Not to any of us.

There are women in scripture like Shiphrah and Puah, the daughters of Zelophehad, Lydia, and Joanna—strong, determined, and accomplished. There are female prophets and leaders like Miriam, Deborah, Huldah, and Anna. God is described as a woman in labor, giving birth to creation, and a woman baking bread. Jesus is described as a mother hen who would gather her brood under her wings. And the list goes on.

Yes, we are created in the very image of God. And so was my mother. She just never knew it. Whether we are Christian or Jewish or Muslim or Buddhist or Hindu or New Age, or consciously and deliberately none of the above, it doesn't matter. What matters is that *we* matter to the Divine Feminine, by whatever name we call her, and that we matter to one another. That we, women of all races, cultures, and beliefs, can join one another in the cosmic conversation of healing and stand together. Stand tall.

Because shame is not our sister. And shame never was.

WHAT *Elizabeth* HOPES READERS WILL TAKE AWAY FROM HER STORY

"Shame is the universal language, and by trusting enough to share our own, we become part of a cosmic conversation of healing. Embraced by the Divine Feminine, we, too, can believe deep in our hearts that we are eternally loved. No matter what."

From Elizabeth: Mother's Best Southern Loaf Bread
a gift from my mother, our sister, to you

⋮

This takes four hours from start to finish, so plan the day accordingly. You will need two good quality, coated 5" x 10" bread pans.

2 cups whole milk
1 stick salted butter, cut into pieces
¾ cup sugar
3 teaspoons active (or instant) yeast
¼ cup water, room temperature
1 egg
5 cups bread flour (not packed, but fluffy)
1 teaspoon salt

- Heat the milk until bubbles begin to form around the edges and it seems ready to boil. Watch out because once milk begins to boil, it happens quickly. Take the milk off the burner and add the butter and sugar. Stir until the sugar is melted. Pour into a mixing bowl. Cool until you can stick your finger all the way in without getting burned. Set aside.

- Mix the yeast in the water. Add to the mixing bowl with the cooled milk mixture in it. Add the egg, flour, and salt. Using the paddle attachment of a stand-up mixer, mix for three minutes.

- While mixing, put one cup of water in the microwave. Boil the water, which takes three minutes. Leaving the cup of water in the microwave, place the mixing bowl inside, covered with a dishtowel with a rubber band around the top to keep it airtight. Close the door and wait about one hour (or more, if needed). The mixture should be doubled in size before you take it out.

- Add two more cups of flour, if needed, and mix for two minutes with a dough hook attachment on your mixer. Put a thin layer of flour on the cabinet. Put the dough on it and cut it in half with a sharp knife. (At this point nothing you do to the dough will mess up the bread.) Working with one piece of dough at a time, fold each piece in half, and then fold in half again. Now place the dough, seam side down in the greased bread pan.

- Reheat the water to boiling in your microwave. Keeping the water there, place the bread tins in, covered with a dishtowel. Let them rise for about one and a half hours. The bread must be doubled in size.

- Bake at 350 degrees for thirty minutes. Turn out of the pans immediately.

- Butter and sink your teeth into the best bread you've ever put in your mouth!

IN THE NAME OF THE FATHER
Hollye Dexter

⋮

My mother was fifteen years old when she became pregnant with me in 1963. My teenaged father was a small-time thief and junkie. As you can imagine, the news of my impending arrival horrified my upper-middle-class grandparents. My grandfather made plans to take my mother to Mexico to abort me, but she refused to go. She always told me she had wanted me, the way a fifteen-year-old girl wants things, the way I, at fifteen, wanted desperately to marry the lead guitar player in the band KISS, sending tear-stained letters to his fan club.

When my mother was in her ninth month of pregnancy, my grandfather, in a drunken rage, pushed her backward into a bathtub, then threw my grandmother on top of her swollen belly. Maybe he imagined a *Gone with the Wind* tumbling-down-the-stairs type of miscarriage. I, however, was a determined fetus.

Over the years, pieces of my story have come to me through different relatives. I was told that on the eve of John F. Kennedy's assassination, my grandmother kicked my grandfather out for good. Shortly thereafter, as the nation mourned the death of Camelot, I was born. It was a traumatic birth, requiring an emergency cesarean for my then sixteen-year-old mother. My father was in jail. No cheery announcements were sent. The family moved away to a remote town in California and kept this shameful secret—*me*—under wraps.

It's not as though anyone had directly told me I was a shameful secret. They didn't need to. Children absorb human emotion like sponges. Shame was imprinted on my soul before I was old enough to know what it was, and I would spend the rest of my life apologizing for it.

As a young child, I did everything I could to deflect that reality. I smiled, I charmed, I danced for company. I pleased my mother, my family members, and even strangers. I never said no. To anyone. My mother said I was the perfect child.

Although the feeling of shame had always hovered around me like an aura, when I was five years old, I found out officially that I was not supposed to be here. On my first day of kindergarten, as my mother walked me toward the office to enroll, she stopped, crouched down at my eye level, and said these words to me:

From now on, you are never to tell anyone your real name. Your father is a bad man in prison, and we are never going to talk about him. As of today, you are Hollye Holmes.

But I wasn't Hollye Holmes. I was Hollye Fisher. That was my name. It's what I was called in nursery school, what it said on my birth certificate, which would remain hidden. Holmes was her new boyfriend's last name, and although they would never marry and he, like all the others, would leave us, she and I used that name for the next two decades.

I walked into the kindergarten classroom that day, my head hung in shame.

Fisher. That was the F-word. That was *me*. The name would forever send me into an inner panic. Even hearing someone talk about fishermen would make my stomach clench with anxiety. Any name that started with F, in fact. I never had a friend growing up whose name started with an F. Upon meeting a new kid, simply hearing the name Freddy, Francis, Felicia was enough to make me clam up. It was a painful reminder that I descended from a bad man and my birth was a terrible mistake.

And so, as children do, I compensated. All my life I tried to *earn* my right to be alive on the planet. I learned to excel. I won spelling bees, got straight A's, could sing, act, dance, paint . . . anything to prove that, although I came from a bad man, I was at least half-okay. I learned to reflect well on my mother—making her proud was the surefire way to win her love.

At nine years old, heavy with the burden of shame, and having lived through more of my mother's poor choices in men, I attempted suicide. I awoke early one morning and calmly decided enough was enough. Wearing ruffled pajamas, I walked into traffic on a major boulevard.

Luckily the drivers were alert that day, and my mother, hearing the screeches, ran out and dragged me into the house. She was terribly disappointed in me. What had happened to her perfect child who always pleased? I had become a problem. Shortly thereafter, I was sent to live with my aunt.

When I returned home a year later, I squashed my feelings down so as not to alienate myself from my mother again. She was all I had, and estrangement was a punishment I could not bear.

I would spend the next thirty years of my life hiding my shame, pushing away from the truth of who I was and what I felt. I went with that new identity she had given me. Hollye Holmes didn't have a bad man for a father. Hollye Holmes wasn't a mistake who was supposed to be aborted. Hollye Holmes could be anyone she wanted. Successful, happy, even loved.

When I was a teenager, my mother worked nights as a waitress in a nightclub. We bought our groceries with food stamps. But Hollye Holmes was a cheerleader and wore the right clothes and had lots of friends. (That is, until all the friends' parents found out where her mother worked.)

Still, Hollye Holmes acted in movies and TV, danced in shows, and sang at concerts. Hollye Holmes excelled in school. Hollye Holmes married the man of her dreams and had beautiful children and built a successful business. But Hollye Holmes was a fractured girl who could never sustain anything good. Anxiety attacks would chase her all her life, as Hollye Fisher was screaming to come out.

And so I straddled the line between the ambassador self I presented to the world, and the self I pushed down to the inner dark places in my soul, that rich self who had so much to tell me, so many gifts to bestow upon me if only I would stop running from my own shadow. But it took me a very long time to stop being afraid.

Living in fear gave shame the reins on my life. It's so easy to see now. The panic attacks in college, when I would sit paralyzed in my car, nauseous, unable to breathe. I knew I didn't belong among the best and brightest. I wasn't clean like them. I was tainted, an imposter. The anxiety plagued me to the point where I was running from class to vomit. I dropped out. Shame won.

There were countless times I was on stage singing, sparkling in sequins in front of hundreds of people. But I knew who I really was, and as I took in their faces looking up at me, I was sure they all knew, too. I suffered terrible stage fright because of it.

I remember one incident in New York when I knew I had been found out. In the early 1990s, I had a children's clothing company that was carried in upscale boutiques and department stores. A group of friends and I had just walked through Manhattan to see my designs on display in the window of Barney's. It was a thrilling moment, a high point in my life. My friend Jack took a picture of us in front of the window, and said casually, "Hollye, you look like a little ragamuffin, lost in the middle of New York City."

I think he was referring to the fact that I was wearing jeans with torn knees, which were the fashion then, but I was so mortified, I actually cried (and I am not, for the record, a public crier). His wife Carrie made him apologize to me, but it wasn't what he said. It was that he saw through me to the truth. *Bingo,* Jack. Inside, that's exactly who I was—white trash, the poor kid from the wrong side of the tracks, the kid who isn't even supposed to exist. And here I was standing in front of Barney's New York. What nerve!

When I was about thirty, I was reading my kids a Dr. Suess book called *Thidwick the Thickhearted Moose* about a gentle moose who allows rude, imposing woodland pests to take up residence in his antlers until he can hardly hold his head up from the weight of them. He almost dies of starvation because he can't migrate with the others. As I read, I fought back tears.

"Why are you crying Mommy?" my son asked.

I gave him some excuse about allergies, and wondered what the hell was wrong with me. Later in talking about it with my husband I realized—I was Thidwick. Those tears were recognition. In my own "antlers," I carried the shame my mother brought to her parents. I carried the shame of my father's heinous past. I carried the shame of things strangers had done to me as a child. It was their shame, not mine. Yet they each took up residence in my head, weighing me down, until it was threatening my life. Recognizing the shame, that vague feeling of worthlessness that had plagued me all my life, was a first step. But it would take me almost two more decades to figure out how to let it go.

I continued to *earn* my right to exist. I was the volunteer mom, the troop leader, the little league mom, the performer, the achiever. And in the quiet of the night I paced the house, anxious, haunted by my own ghosts. One Christmas, my husband bought me a beautiful little change purse filled with Tums, the antacids I popped like candy on a daily basis. This simple gesture touched me so deeply, it brought tears to my eyes. He knew me. He knew I paced and my stomach wretched and I tried to hide it. He knew, and he loved me anyway. Every time he hugged me he would say, "You are nothing but good, Baby. Pure good." And I wanted so badly to believe him, but there was this Hollye Fisher girl inside of me. I didn't know her, but I hated her. I reviled and rejected her.

People had always asked where my father was, and *didn't I want to find out?* No. I did not. Being the obedient girl I was, I never spoke about my father, and in fact, I believed my mother when she told me he was dead. I buried him in my mind, and with him, I buried that part of me. It was *soul murder*—I thought I could get away with it.

But he wasn't dead. By the time I was thirty-nine years old, I had fallen into a deep depression. The past had chased me to a state of exhaustion, and I collapsed, waving the white flag. My husband strongly encouraged me to find out who I really was. *Find your father,* he said. *Find him.* Since no photographs existed of my father, and no one in my family would speak of him, I had always secretly feared I was the product of rape or incest. Now I had to know. After all, could the truth be any worse than my own imaginings?

With the help of my husband and a genealogist, I did find my father, and to my surprise, it was not the nightmare I'd expected, but a joyful reunion. He was out of state, but for the next two months we spoke on the phone every day as I slowly gathered the pieces of my history. My father had spent my entire childhood in prison. The enormity of that truth was hard for me to absorb. I would find out that while I was a nine-year-old girl throwing myself into traffic, he was sitting in isolation in a San Quentin prison cell, reading the Bible. He'd been living the straight life in Texas for over twenty years, and he was now a Baptist preacher, admired and respected by everyone in town. I also found out I had three brothers (who would soon become the loves of my life).

On Thanksgiving 2003, I flew out to meet him. The moment we locked eyes at the airport, I knew I was his child. I *was* Hollye Fisher. He wrapped his arms around me as I trembled uncontrollably, using everything in me to keep that Fisher girl under wraps as she tried to emerge to her father.

We stayed up late that night talking, and he told me something that would change me forever—one simple sentence. *You were conceived in love.*

Not hate.

Not rape.

Love.

Puppy love, perhaps, but some kind of love nonetheless. How awful could I be if I came from love? I felt something shift inside me, all the way down to a cellular level. The heavy blanket of shame was lifting.

He said he and my mother had run away from home in Burbank, California, boarding a Greyhound bus for Texas, where they planned to marry. But my grandparents had them hunted down. The sheriff pulled the bus over in Stockton and took the two young indigents to jail, where they held hands through the bars and talked until the sun came up, planning their idyllic future together, a future that would be marred by drugs and pain and loss. As he told me these stories, he held my hand. It was the first time in my life I had held my father's hand, and I realized I didn't even know what they looked like. I looked down to study them, those hands that held me as a baby, hands that held the bible in a prison cell, hands that painted the stormy seas that now hung over my mantel—my father's hands. That's when I saw the tattoo: *Aryan Nation*. My stomach lurched. I thought I would vomit. Here it was all over again: the fear, the shame, the nightmare of being me. *Who is this man that I descend from?*

This time, I didn't run from the truth. I had come this far—I had to know. I found the courage to ask the hard questions. The writer in me was riveted, committing every word to memory. The daughter in me wanted to turn back the clock and pretend I never asked, but I had to face it now—every word of it.

In San Quentin, he explained, you join a gang for protection, or you die. Or worse. He, being white, had no choice but to join the Aryan Brotherhood. He had to fight with them in prison riots, knifing his friends, the black and hispanic guys he joked around with at his kitchen job during the day. If you didn't show allegiance to your own gang, they'd kill you themselves. I knew nothing of this world. I grew up a poor little hippie kid in the flower-power sixties, knowing no color lines.

I asked why he hadn't had the tattoo removed. *How can you preach love from the pulpit with hate on your hands?* I asked.

I don't erase it because it's part of my life story. I have to live with the truth of my past.

Say what you will about my father, but he never ran from the truth. Everyone in town knows his history. His employers know he is an ex-con. He mentors kids—black, Hispanic, white—and tells them his story. I've sat in his Bible study classes, next to Hispanics who listen to him with reverence. They see the Aryan Nation tattoo on his hand, the hand that now reaches out to them. He wears his scars and shame out in the open, every day.

I writhe inside from it. It makes me sick. I wanted him to erase it, or at the very least transform it. I don't agree with his decision to keep this ugliness tattooed on his body, but I have to accept that this is his life, his decision, to bare his scars. It is a reminder of his shame, not mine.

I now held the truth, the precious, devastating truth, in my hands. It had shattered me, or at least the persona I had tried to build. I was too exhausted to run from it any more. And so I began to tell my story—all of it, to anyone who asked. I wrote a memoir. Then I wrote another. I started a blog about living in truth. Eventually, it broke me open and rewarded me in ways I never could have imagined. Not everyone, however, greeted my newfound growth with cheers and open arms. My mother and I have been estranged now for almost a decade. One of the last things she said to me before breaking off communication: *shame on you.*

But I am not shame. I am not my father. I am not my mother. I am no longer the young, weak girl who made poor decisions. I am not the summation of my mistakes. I am not the grief or the judgment cast upon me by others. I am not the mistake my parents made, nor the tears shed by my grandparents.

Inside me is a spirit, bright and thriving, that was made by the Creator of this world. I have looked into the eyes of a newborn child. I know our Creator doesn't make mistakes.

I am not a mistake.

I am Hollye Fisher.

I am shameless.

WHAT *Hollye* HOPES READERS WILL TAKE AWAY FROM HER STORY

"Each of our lives is a miracle, every one of us is meant to be here, and we are all equally important cogs in the wheel of life."

BITS & PIECES FOR FIVE HUNDRED
Amy Ferris

. . .

Shame, to me, was worn as an accessory.

I would wear it like a piece of jewelry, sometimes it would lay on my shoulder like a pin, sometimes it was a wool scarf wrapped around my neck, sometimes it was an afterthought, like a snazzy belt or a bold silver necklace. But it seems, as I write this now, that for most of my life I wore shame, not even knowing where or how it originated.

I was maybe five, maybe six, I don't remember the exact age, but I do remember the screaming and yelling.

They were always fighting.

Loud, yelling, and screaming.

"Go to hell, Sam."

"No, you, you go to hell, Bea."

Their bedroom was across from mine. I could always hear them, cursing each other. I was never sure what it was they were fighting, arguing about, but it always escalated, and by the time I was deep under the covers I could barely make out who was screaming at whom.

Their voices blending.

The calling each other bad, nasty names. My very first "show and tell" at school, where I actually stood up, and told something, was a dirty joke. Literally, I stood up in front of my class, in a frilly little dress, and told a dirty joke. My teacher was mortified. Horrified.

"What can a bird do that a man can't do?" I asked enthusiastically to the entire classroom of eight-year-olds.

"Whistle through its pecker," I answered to the now wide-eyed audience.

None, not one kid, got the joke. When my mother came to school to pick me up, the teacher reported that I had both an unusual vocabulary, and a dirty, filthy mouth. My mother said she wasn't surprised since both she and my father cursed a great deal. I was put on word probation. If I'm not mistaken, my teacher even recommended washing my mouth out with soap, but there were limits to what my mother would do in relationship to punishment.

This particular night my mother was louder than usual. I don't remember the gist of it, but at around 2:00 AM, she scooped me out of bed, in my pajamas, and carried me out to the car. I caught sight of my father standing in the doorway, unable to prevent her from storming off. She placed me on the back seat, where I was both groggy and scared. My mother drove to the Empress Diner, a short trip from our home, where she ordered rice pudding and coffee. That night, the back booth, faux (hard) leather seats and all, became our home. I curled up, while my mother chain-smoked.

"Why we here, Mommy? Why we here?"

"Because your father is a shit."

"What's that mean, Mommy? What's that mean?"

She lit one cigarette after another, and the combination of the smoke and the rice pudding and fried foods lingered much longer than those few hours.

I suspect she reached a point—or maybe she ran out of cigarettes—where she no longer wanted to sit in that booth at the diner. Or maybe, just maybe (in hindsight), she felt she had punished him enough. When we finally pulled into our driveway, and I shuffled into the house, it was my father's face I vividly remember. It was almost cinematic; sitting in his favorite chair in the living room—a blue corduroy chair—tucked into the corner, his eyes filled with deep, penetrating sadness. Maybe he didn't think we'd come back home. I'm quite sure this wasn't the first time my mother stormed out, ran out, left him worrying, wondering. But this was the first time she took me with her, the first time I saw and heard the thud of shame. It was filled with apologizing; "I'm sorry," said over and over and over again. It was bending over backward. It was filled with tremendous fear and worry and the words, please . . . I'm begging you, repeated like a mantra.

My father's shame was not that he had done something wrong; it was the shame of not being able to stand up to my mother who intentionally hurt him. Her cruelty kept him worried sick for hours and hours. His shame came from cowardice.

I would remember that shame and tuck it away, and wear it on many occasions growing up.

A few years later, a god-awful event occurred in my family. A holy-shit event. My father was arrested, all went boom.

My father worked for the IRS as an auditor.

He took a bribe.

He was caught.

He was arrested.

It was that simple. It was horrific and scary. Memories of it, bits and pieces, flood my brain, but I don't have the full picture. I don't know the full honest-to-goodness story. I never asked. I didn't want to know. And no one, not one person talked about it. I just remember him being led away, but then there are big blurs—holes in the story—that follow. I remember the financial struggles, the pawning of jewelry, the loss of friends. I remember my mother stoic, my father sullen. My family, including relatives, managed to keep that buried and hidden. At first, my dad was convicted on something like four counts, and then it was overturned. Maybe he had a good lawyer. Maybe he knew the judge. Obviously, those are the bullet points, the quick summary, the straight and narrow story. From there, shame found a way of moving in with us; it was there, right there, sitting at the table, for each and every meal; lounging on the couch while we watched TV; sitting next to me while I did my homework, hovering while we slept. It was not talked about, or discussed, but it was palpable.

The word shame became a favorite, even winning over "fuck you" and "go to hell."

If I did something, or said something that my mother didn't particularly like, or approve of, she would berate me, hurt me, dismiss me, saying, "Shame on you, shame on you, shame on you" and yes, I would actually believe that I was shameful. That along with her other favorite mantra, "God will punish you," made me all set for a sinful life.

Between God and shame, I was pretty much sure that I didn't have a chance in hell.

Shame is insidious. It can masquerade as arrogance, or distance, or self-sabotage. It is heartbreaking and heart-stopping. It keeps so much buried. It keeps everyone at arm's length. Like a bit too much perfume, it lingers even after you leave the room.

I was twelve. My dad was working in New York City at a place called Melvin's Frame Shop somewhere in midtown Manhattan. A far fall from where he had been a few years earlier. He was both a provider and a hard worker, and this was the only job he could get while awaiting trial. Melvin was a holocaust survivor, and was cruel and vicious and I often wondered if he had always been so very cruel to the bone, or if his experience at Auschwitz made him a punisher, particularly toward his Jewish friends and comrades. He treated my father like dirt. I often went with my dad to work on Saturdays, where Melvin bullied and belittled him, as I watched what little self-worth my father had left get brushed away—along with the dirt and the dust—into the corners on the floor he was sweeping.

On the ride home—the Long Island Railroad, New York/Massapequa line—we would sit together, and I would often grab hold of my dad's hand and squeeze it so hard in hopes that I could squeeze the bad day and the bad man out of him. He seemed so defeated. So small. He was no longer the big, strong, joyful man whose shoes I would dance on, or whose shoulder I would rest my head on. He was filled with sorrow and shame and the weight of the world.

I tucked that shame away, too, letting others bully me and squash my hopes. And just like my dad, I would wear it and suck it in, and silently pray to be given an opportunity to prove my worth.

My dad rebounded. He got back on his feet. And though he rebuilt his life and created fortune over the years, he wore the shame of his past life like a heavy coat, and in the pockets, he carried the sad and lingering side effect of his inability to forgive himself.

He never forgave himself.

He lived with regret.

And my mother, God bless her soul, managed to add the layer of entitlement to her wardrobe, the piece worn that made her believe she was better than, superior to others.

I, too, inherited all of these pieces—an entire wardrobe of shame, guilt, fear, doubt, worry, and self-hatred. Passed down through experience, memory, words, actions, glimpses. Mothers to daughters, fathers to sons, fathers to daughters, and mothers to sons.

I dropped out of school, I did drugs, I slept with a lot of the wrong guys. I made wrong turns and gigantic mistakes, and I hurt myself and others through my actions, deeds, and words.

Not surprising.

Not surprising one bit.

After years and years of living off that inheritance, that trust fund (or mistrust fund), I found myself no longer fitting into the old habits. Everything began to feel too tight, too uncomfortable. It's as if one day I woke up and decided that it was time to stop bullying myself. I no longer wanted to lug around the shopping bags of a self-slandering life.

✳

This is where the *happily ever after* part comes in.

We all carry shame.

We all, each of us, carry shame, and wear it like a corsage. On a lapel, on our wrist; or on a slender strap. And it was within that simple sentence—we all carry shame—that a lifetime of bits and pieces were able to find a home, a safe haven, where they could become whole. A place where I could thread a tapestry together, and understand that all that I am and feel and experience has been linked through moments of deep shame. Not just my own shame, but my mother's and my father's—our shame—intertwined.

And through friendship, love, and trust, that moment of shedding all that we were taught, all the misguided beliefs we carry, a sense of mission manifested. Grew. Blossomed.

My mother often said to me, "Amy, let's keep this our secret," as if by doing that, the secrets would never resurface. They would be cremated alongside my father and her. And as all good girls do, I, too, believed that keeping her secrets—our secrets—would make me a better daughter, a good daughter. A daughter worthy of love.

I was wrong.

Wholly wrong.

In the de-cluttering, and de-layering of my shame wardrobe, I found memories, trinkets, bits, and pieces of *me* filled with goodness, miracles, and magic. Love and kindness. I never chose to look at that side. I was so faithful to being my parents' child that I failed to acknowledge the woman I had become. It is only through releasing the secrets, sharing the shame, and telling the story so that others are able to "find their way home" that I finally understand the power, the magnificence, and the pure magic of self-love.

WHAT *Amy* HOPES READERS WILL TAKE AWAY FROM HER STORY

"I hope people stand up—strong and bright—and light the way for someone else. I hope that we stop saying *shame on you* and start saying *good for you*. I hope that in sharing our stories—our fears and sorrows and crippling self-doubt—that we shed all that keeps us small, distant, and at arm's length. I hope that in sharing these stories, we give other human beings courage and hope and a place to call home. I hope within these pages, within all these words, that it is made clear that we no longer need permission to speak our glorious truth."

1329 LYNX TRAIL

Samantha Dunn

⋮

At 1329 Lynx Trail, a kind of zoo has been waiting for me for almost a year. Cat puke, dog piss, fuzz bunnies, dust mites. Mold, mildew, fungus. Fleas. Oh yes, fleas. These are the final inhabitants of my mom's house.

The truth is—and this is just one of the many, many things I don't want to talk about regarding 1329 Lynx Trail, I mean, *at all*—they also lived there when she lived there.

Now they have outlived her.

They were the reason I hadn't gone back home to New Mexico to see her in more than seven years, preferring to send her an airline ticket to L.A. a couple of times a year instead. I'd routinely get calls from her neighbors at the mobile home park, once from an old college friend, once from a paramedic there on an emergency call when she had a small stroke. The calls would go something like:

"Well, I don't know how to tell you this" [sad, awkward pause] "but it's about your mom. Her house—"

"I know."

I'm good at cutting people off. I can summon a thunderous tone of finality you don't want to mess with. I learned it from Mom.

Person-on-the-Phone will hesitate on the other end of the line.

"It's just that it's really bad, I mean unhealthy—"

"I *know.*"

Again with the awkward silence.

Then, a timid offering: "It just seems like something should/could/can be done—"

I would hear this one sentence several ways, all at once. I would hear, "You should be a better daughter and not let your mother live in a house so filthy it's not fit for swine." And hear, "Why haven't you done anything?" And hear, "What's wrong with you people?" *What'swrongwithyoupeople, what'swrongwithyoupeople.*

"If it were possible for me to do anything, I would. I have tried. Believe me," I would say in clipped, frosty syllables.

Sometimes at this point in the conversation I would tell Person-on-the-Phone the story of the cat food. How I had been out to see Mom, staying in the far back room, the one that was the tiny outpost of relative cleanliness. How after she had left for her shift at the hospital in the morning, I came out to the kitchen to get coffee—Mom made great coffee—and realized I couldn't possibly drink, let alone eat, out of anything in the kitchen. So I had the bright idea to clean it while she was gone. Let me back up and say that she'd bellow and rage if I so much as moved a cat hair off the couch before I sat down, so I'd learned to voice my disapproval and discomfort through eye rolls and sneering comments.

I started with the prep island in the center of the room because it seemed the most manageable—stacks of mail, crumbs, bags of moldy bread, rotten bananas. A mountain of cat food heaped up from an automatic feeder. The feeder had long since quit working, so Mom had taken to pouring Meow Mix in a pile around the general area. She also dumped on cans of tuna, which had ossified into globs of stink. I took some paper towels and began to sweep the mountain into a Hefty bag when I noticed small, white bits of the food undulating. I pushed the mountain harder and the crust fell away. There, exposed, lay a mass of squirming maggots.

Maggots. In the kitchen.

I screamed and ran outside. Then I started to cry. I don't mean cry. I mean sobs shook me so hard I thought I'd crack a rib. Tears scalded my face and I must have howled, because some retirees walking by with their fluffy-assed shih tzu stopped and stared.

"What?" I screamed at them. "What. Are. You. Looking. At."

Taking out emotions on objects and random strangers is a common reflex in my family, but this time it made me feel no better. It did, however, make me realize I needed to pull it together. So I went inside, picked my way through the sticky, warped yellow pages I found in a stack under the end table where Mom kept her phone, and called an industrial cleaning service.

Some $700 and five hours later, a super-powered janitorial team had rendered most of the house habitable, if not downright spic-and-span in most areas. Her bedroom and master bath were still a little dicey but I'd run out of money, so it would have to do. I lit some incense. I started sweeping the porch just in time for her red Chevy to pull up in the driveway.

I was anxious but excited for her to see inside. Did I think she would turn to me like I was the Great White Hope and tell me how grateful she was? How she had desperately needed help but didn't know how to ask for it? That starting right here, right now, things would be different, a fresh start, a new leaf, and all of the other clichés? I am ashamed to say, yes, all of that is exactly what I wished for.

What she did instead was look around, bewildered. Then her face, that lightly freckled redhead skin, started to redden. "Jesus H. Christ," she seethed with an anger that was beyond anger, a blast of fury so much worse than the volcanic kind. "What the hell have you done? Who the fuck did you let in here? Goddammit, you have no right—"

"Don't you like it?" was the first thing I said before it all went to hell and I got defensive, told her to go screw herself, that she was a drunk and she could just live in a sty for the rest of her life for all I cared. I said things like that back then. I vowed I would never again do one damn thing to her house, and I didn't. Ever. Not one thing.

I realize now that she must have felt ambushed, exposed. She must have felt profoundly embarrassed, humiliated in fact, to have anyone see the evidence of how not in control she was of life in general and hers in particular.

※

Let me back up further and explain that my mom—Deanne was her name—was certifiably brilliant, with an IQ of 165. She worked as an emergency room and operating room nurse before she went into nursing management. She had served in the Air Force and for all her life retained that commanding way, as if she had entered a room just to give orders. With a cigarettes-and-booze, Peggy Lee voice and a Shirley McLaine look, she did not suffer the company of idiots. Mom was born in the Chinese year of the tiger but I always thought of her as more armadillo; a leathery exterior covering a soft, pink interior. I didn't know much about that interior—no one did—but I knew it was there from the touch of her hand to my forehead when I was sick, the cool brush of her lips to my cheek, the way she talked baby talk to cats and faithfully watered her lush houseplants. A love of poetry and music and novels was like a deep underground river that nourished her; her nose was always in a book.

The houses we lived in when I was a child were subaverage clean, what you'd expect of a home of three women on the ragged hem of the middle class, a single mother working full time, a self-involved daughter, a grandmother whose problems it would take a psychiatrist to diagnose because I can't explain her. There was booze. Money troubles. Man troubles.

The descent into pathologic filth didn't begin until 1989, the year I returned to the States after living in France because my stepdad, the man my mom had finally found happiness with, was sick. That was the year he died of AIDS, then my grandfather of brain cancer, my great-uncle of a heart attack, my grandmother of a stroke. Yes. All in one year. Mom, always a boozer, now began to drink with a more terrifying virulence. It was like watching her shove a loaded gun into her mouth day after day. I fled to L.A. with an old boyfriend-destined-to-be-ex-husband.

All I could think about was what I had lost, but I did not stop to do the math on my mom's losses. Gone now was the loving husband she had waited a lifetime to finally meet, both her parents, her uncle. And me, her only child, now far away, bitter, judgmental, always peeved about something.

So if the dog peed on the carpet, whatever. Spilled a little tomato sauce on the linoleum? Who's around to notice? Dust once and it will come right back again tomorrow, so what's the point? And so began the accumulation.

I knew from the concerned phone calls that the situation was beyond terrible, but I also knew it from the fact that every time she came to see me she looked a little worse. It was a slow erosion. She was thinner by degrees. More haggard. My mom was always showy as a peacock but little rips started appearing in her clothes, holes in her shoes. A couple of years ago on one of her visits, I came into the bathroom when she was undressing and saw that her skin was covered in a red rash and welts. I guessed flea bites, bedbugs. She looked—my god, what is the word? Fragile. This woman who had once held together the half-blown, bloody skull of a patient in her hands so his brains might not spill, who had delivered babies and knew how to suture skin like silk, this woman who never seemed to suffer a moment of doubt, looked fragile.

I remember tears again rising and the urge to yell at her, to say, *why the hell are you like this?* But by then I had had years of therapy, sat zazen with a Buddhist roshi, practiced yoga, had a Catholic priest as a buddy, belonged to a couple of twelve-step programs. Most days I still had the urge to beat something, but I didn't. I don't know if it was some kind of enlightenment or just age that had begun to grow seeds of compassion in my anemic soil.

"Mommy," I said. I know it's weird for a woman my age to call her mother Mommy but I did sometimes. I came up and hugged her tight. "I love you. I wish you loved you like I love you."

She didn't pull away or make a joke.

"I love you, too, babydoll," she said.

She even let me put cortizone cream on her back. Then she said something about the rash and being allergic to the Bounce fabric softeners and my semi-enlightenment dimmed.

I said with that acid kind of sarcasm, "Oh no it can't have *anything* to do with the toxic levels of cat hair or dog shit in your house. *Oh nooo,*" and there we were, at it again.

Here's the paradox: She collected cleaning items. She must have owned four vacuums. Had a forest of products under the sinks in the kitchen and bathrooms. Simple Green, Ajax, Pine Sol, Windex. She was forever clipping coupons to lure me from the generic cleaners I use, and she swore by Tide detergents. She sent in for products from infomercials—green bags to keep produce from rotting, Sham-Wow rags to mop spills—and had them delivered to my house. I considered it just one of her many eccentricities, like the gold-lamé, leopard-print evening gown she owned. Now, though, thinking about it chokes me up to the point where I feel like I might drown and then makes me want to sleep, but I can't sleep because whenever I shut my eyes, images of her and her house flood my brain.

So I guess I should tell you what happened.

Last August, she told me over the phone that she had stepped on a piece of glass in her kitchen. She said she had broken a cup and thought she'd swept up the shards, but had obviously missed a few. The fact that she was telling me this in one of our daily check-in calls should have been a warning, should have been a call to action, because when did she ever bother with a detail like that? Never. She'd once fallen against a kitchen counter and sliced her nose open so deeply she had a scar running over her face in a crescent for the rest of her days, but didn't mention the incident until I picked her up at the airport and said, "So what's with the new nose job?"

Again a month later, she said the air conditioning had gone out in her house—in her New Mexico town, the summer heat is always in the triple digits—and mentioned the cut on her foot. She said she was having trouble getting the wound to heal so she had gone to see a doctor friend who had given her antiobitics. This is where my concern started. She thought doctors on the whole were shysters and quacks, to be consulted only when other options had been exhausted. For her to go to one, even to a friend, was tantamount to Custer raising the surrender flag. Still, I didn't ask questions, or fly her out to see me or, God forbid, go out to her to help.

If you'd asked me about it, I would have told you it was an Al-Anon thing about keeping my own side of the street clean or a Buddhist idea of nonattachment or some other horseshit lingo. I think the mean, dark truth of it was that I wanted to be right.

I wanted to say, "See Mom? See what happens when you drink like a fish and your house is a sty?"

Maybe, even, I wanted to get back at her for all the times I had felt embarrassed by her behavior as a child and as a teenager and, oh Christ, even as a forty-year-old woman. All the times people had looked askance, all the times I wanted to yell, "But I'm not like her! Don't judge me!"

She was seventy-two years old, walked like she was on the deck of a rocking boat, her right hand shook with a faint palsey, and yet this was the kind of pathetic shit that occupied me and my overinflated sense of myself.

So finally I send her a ticket to come spend the holidays. It was October. My toddler son and I walked right by her in the airport. I didn't even recognize her. She'd lost a good twenty pounds. She limped badly.

"If I was a horse, you'd have to shoot me," she quipped as I took her bags and tried to steady her.

"Can I shoot you anyway?"

This was actually our normal code for "I am happy to see you" and "I am so glad you're here, Mom," but now I wish we had just said that.

Things got bad, and fast.

The "cut" turned out to be a hole in the bottom of her foot that was the size of a fifty-cent piece; bone and tendon exposed. Of course we're talking gangrene, emergency surgery. Half her foot had to be amputated. It was determined she suffered cirrhosis, and blocked arteries. A secondary infection set in. Her system went septic. Her body shut down.

On January 10, 2011, I sat in the ICU unit as she lay comatose. I held her hand, watched her let out one long breath and a shrug as if to say, "Is that all there is?" She died just two days short of her birthday.

December. For almost a year, a new kind of call has come from Person-on-the-Phone, asking, "When are you coming to New Mexico to take care of your mother's house?" And for almost a year I have said I do not have the money to deal with it. Neither my husband nor I can take the time off work. I can't leave my three-year-old for so long.

All of that has been true. But what I have been too ashamed to say to Person-on-the-Phone or to my friends or my husband or even myself, is that the real problem is: I cannot go back to that house and see what she, the mother I loved, lived within, and what I let her live within. I cannot smell the overpowering ammonia of urine from long-gone-dogs that saturates the carpets and know she must have smelled the same asphyxiating smell. I cannot see the grime on the linoleum kitchen floor and not search for the blood left when the glass shard went into her foot. 1329 Lynx Trail is a kind of crime scene in my mind.

What have I done? What have I done?

January. Because I could not sleep, because my sadness was becoming a wet blanket wrapping my entire family, because we had to, my husband cashed a retirement account, our son stayed with his babysitter and her two kids, and we stole four days from our life to return to 1329 Lynx Trail.

In the first moment, yes, the pain of seeing the place had been as ferocious as I had imagined. Quickly, though, and for every moment after, a feeling not unlike happiness filled me. Underneath the layer of filth is the world that made me, the things of the mother I loved. Everywhere—from the framed photos of us and of me throughout the house to the innumerable postcards I had sent her from my travels made into a collage covering the fridge, my books on her shelves, the articles of mine she had photocopied and evidently handed out to people she met—everywhere I found the evidence that she had known she was loved.

Evidence: I did what I could.

So a funny thing happened: I was in 1329 Lynx Trail alone for the first time, my husband having run to the store on an errand. I was in the living room going through her mail. High upon the wall opposite the room was an annoying clock whose chintzy, piercing chimes had tinned the hour too loud for as long as I could remember. I'd always told Mom how much I hated that clock.

"Mom, that thing is so ugly and it's making me deaf," I'd say. "And besides, you're retired! Why the hell do you need to know what hour it is? It's like *For Whom the Bell Tolls* or something. Christ."

And of course that just made her more committed to leaving it on the wall.

I was reading the mail, and all of a sudden, in the middle of the day, when not even a breeze was stirring, I heard a crash. In front of me, the hated clock had spontaneously fallen to the floor and broken apart. Nothing else fell. Nothing else moved.

My husband suspected that the nail had not been placed in a stud and had finally given way. Surprised it hadn't happened years ago, in fact. I nodded my head, but inside I will know what she was saying: You did all you could do.

WHAT *Samantha* HOPES READERS WILL TAKE AWAY FROM HER STORY

"You are not the only one."

ABUNDANT GRATITUDE
Amy and Hollye wish to thank:

⋮

All of the courageous women who wrote for this book, for pushing beyond their own personal limits, through their own pain and discomfort, to share the most powerful moments of their lives.

Jill Marsal and Krista Lyons for believing in this project.

Kristine Van Raden and Victoria Zackheim for their tremendous generosity of spirit, sharing ideas, inspiration, and advice (true examples of women supporting women).

All our Facebook girlfriends on the ferris wheel for cheering us on from start to finish.

FROM *Amy*

My gratitude list is so very long; the generosity of my friends and family is just so enormous. To all my girlfriends (and boyfriends) for always, always keeping me warm on the cold bitter days, for keeping me cool on the hot, sticky days, and for always making me believe in the goodness and kindness and magic out in the world.

Peter, Frances, Marvin, Marcia G., Barbara, Robyn, Sean, Xavier, Laura, Nancy, Florin, Amy L., Bob, Suzanne, Jody, Michael, Brenda, Sam, Liz, Karen, Jeffrey, Victoria, Krista, Troy, Amy F., Ronnie Biondo, Gloria Feldt, Teresa, Tom, Liza, and Maleyne, I thank you all for loving me, believing in me.

To my parents for being imperfect, unintentionally allowing me to navigate my way in this crazy, gorgeous world so that I was able to find and love me. For Hollye Dexter, because collaboration coupled with friendship is truly the icing on the cake, and for Ken who loves me unconditionally and forgives me my bad days.

FROM *Hollye*

Thank you, from the bottom of my heart, to all the people who were by my side through the process of making this book happen.

My husband, Troy, for being my support system, my cheerleader, and my best friend.

Amy Ferris for being the Muse and the Dreamcatcher, for weekly spirit-lifts and pep-talks, for being the best collaborative partner and friend a girl could hope for.

Erin Doyle and Beth Eisenberg, and Dani Robinson and the kids for being my family, my heart, and a constant source of support and belief in me.

Aunt Diane, for helping me to find my father.

My father Ted Fisher for his honesty.

Bernard Selling for years of stewarding my writing, Joyce Maynard for nudging me out into the world, Monica Holloway for cheering me on every step of the way.

My children, Cristen, Taylor, and Evan, and my grandbaby Ayumu for filling my world with love and chaos.

And finally, special thanks to every therapist I've ever had (you know who you are).

SHAMELESS WOMEN

BROOKE ELISE AXTELL is an award-winning writer, performing artist, and media consultant. She is a passionate advocate for survivors of gender violence. As a member of the speakers bureau for *Rape, Abuse, Incest, National Network* and the founder of *Survivor Healing and Empowerment*, a healing community for survivors of rape, abuse and sex-trafficking, she speaks about Radical Recovery, the intersection of personal healing and social justice. Brooke is a contributing writer for *ForbesWoman* addressing women's rights and leadership. Her work has been featured in many media outlets, including *Fox News, The San Francisco Chronicle, The Boston Globe, CBS Radio,* and *Pacifica Radio, New York.* You can listen to her new CD, *Creatrix,* and read excerpts from her poetry collection, *Kore of the Incantation,* at http://brookeaxtell.com.

NINA BURLEIGH is a journalist and the author of five books. She is currently working on an ebook single about women and the Arab Spring to be published in March 2012 by Byliner. Her latest book, *The Fatal Gift of Beauty,* was a *New York Times* bestseller. In the last several years, she has profiled a wide array of subjects, including American politicians, Israeli archaeological forgers, an Arab feminist, a small-town Italian mayor murdered over slow food politics, asteroid deflection experts, and Chinese immigrants to Italy. She's written for numerous publications including *Businessweek, The New Yorker, Time, New York, The New Statesman,* and *The New York Times,* and is a contributing editor at *Elle.* She has appeared on *Good Morning America, Nightline, The Today Show, 48 Hours, MSNBC, CNN* and *C-Span,* and on NPR and numerous radio programs. Nina was born and educated in the Midwest, has traveled extensively in the Middle East, and lived in Italy and France.

RACHEL KRAMER BUSSEL (rachelkramerbussel.com) is an author, editor, blogger and event organizer. She has edited over 40 anthologies, including *Dirty Girls, Curvy Girls, Orgasmic, Women in Lust, Gotta Have It, Going Down, Passion, Suite Encounters, The Mile High Club, Anything for You,* and the nonfiction Best Sex Writing series. She writes widely about sex, dating, books, and pop culture, and her work has been published at *The Frisky, Glamour, New York, The Root, Salon, Time Out New York, xoJane,* and elsewhere. She teaches erotic writing workshops and organizes readings around the world. She has appeared on *The Martha Stewart Show, The Gayle King Show,* and others. She co-edits the blog *Cupcakes Take the Cake.* (cupcaketakesthecake.blogspot.com)

HOLLYE DEXTER is coeditor of *Dancing At the Shame Prom,* and recently completed a second memoir, *What Doesn't Kill You.* Her essays have been published in anthologies (*Chicken Soup For the Soul, Answered Prayers,* and *Character Consciousness*) and in many online publications. She writes regularly for iPinion Syndicate and AOL Patch News. A singer/songwriter with four albums out, she also founded the award-winning nonprofit *Art and Soul*, running workshops for teenagers in the foster care system. In 2007 she received the Agape Spirit award from Dr. Michael Beckwith (from *The Secret*) for her work with at-risk youth. Together, Hollye and Amy Ferris teach writing workshops, helping others to find their authentic voices. She is on staff for the San Miguel Writer's Conference and is a visiting author at UCLA extension. She lives in Southern California with her husband and three children, where she hikes, plays music, and blogs about living an authentic life: www.hollyedexter.blogspot.com

SHARON DOUBIAGO After completing her critically acclaimed first book, the epic poem *Hard Country*, Sharon embarked on a bus journey with her fifteen-year-old daughter to Macchu Picchu. *South America Mi Hija* was named the *Best Book of the Year* by the *Los Angeles Weekly*. She has lived much of her life since in three vans— Roses, Psyche, and Valentine—writing full-time rather than working full-time in order to write part-time. Some of this life is chronicled in her prose stories. *The Book of Seeing with One's Eyes* received Gloria Steinem's *Woman Writer Award*, and the title story won a Pushcart Prize for fiction. Her poetry collection, *Body and Soul*, garnered her a third Pushcart Prize. Published chapters from her unfinished memoir *Son* received the Tom Robbin's Journalist of the Year Award ("for the most outrageous, risk-taking, life-affirming article published in the Northwest"). Latest works include *Love on the Streets, Selected and New Poems* and *My Father's Love, Portrait of the Poet as a Girl/Woman, Two Volumes*. She's currently a board member of PEN Oakland and has just completed a new poetry manuscript, *Writing*.

SAMANTHA DUNN is the author of several books, including the novel *Failing Paris*, a finalist for the PEN Center Fiction Award. Her essays have been widely anthologized, including the collection she coedited, *Women on the Edge: Writing from Los Angeles*. She teaches in the UCLA Writers Program and is the adviser for PEN Center's The Mark, a program to help new writers complete finished books.

AMY FERRIS is coeditor of *Dancing at The Shame Prom*. She is an author, editor, screenwriter, and playwright. Her memoir, *Marrying George Clooney, Confessions From a Midlife Crisis* (Seal Press), is Off-Broadway bound. She has contributed to numerous anthologies, and has written everything from young adult novels to films. She co-wrote *Funny Valentines* (Julie Dash, director), and *Mr. Wonderful* (Anthony Minghella, director). *Funny Valentines* was nominated for a best screenplay award and numerous BET awards. She cocreated and coedited the first ever all-women's issue of *Living Buddhism* magazine. She serves on the executive board of directors at The Pages & Places Literary Festival, Peters Valley Arts, Education and Craft Center, and is on the advisory board of The Women's Media Center. She is on faculty at The San Miguel de Allende Writers Conference. She is a visiting teacher at the UCLA Writers Workshop (extension). She contributes regularly to iPinion

Syndicate. Her number one goal, desire, dream is that *all women awaken to their greatness*. You can find her blogging in the middle of the night at: www.marrying-georgeclooney.com. She lives in Pennsylvania with her husband, Ken.

AMY FRIEDMAN writes the internationally syndicated column *Tell Me a Story*, and has published two memoirs and thousands of stories and essays. She teaches memoir and personal essay at UCLA Extension, Skirball Cultural Arts Center, Idyllwild School of the Arts, and in public high schools through PEN USA's Pen in the Classroom. Her recently completed memoir, *Desperado's Wife*, tells the story of her life as a prisoner's wife and her work on behalf of prisoners' families.

ELIZABETH GEITZ is an Episcopal priest, newspaper columnist, and award-winning author of numerous books, including *Soul Satisfaction: Reclaiming the Divine Feminine* and *Gender and the Nicene Creed*. Elizabeth's books have been hailed by people as diverse as Desmond Tutu, John Berendt, and Helen Prejean. Her most recent, *I Am That Child: Changing Hearts and Changing the World,* chronicles her odyssey with two other women of faith to a home for AIDS orphans in Cameroon, West Africa, yielding profound insights into AIDS, the criminalization of homosexuality, and gender and racial discrimination. With a focus on women's spirituality and justice, Elizabeth's writings speak to people of passion who want to make a difference in the world. She lives in the Delaware Highlands of Pennsylvania with her husband, Michael. Visit her at www.elizabethgeitz.com.

COLLEEN HAGGERTY is a woman in her early fifties who cares less and less about the issues that used to bring her so much shame. As an ambassador for the Prosthetics Outreach Foundation, Colleen created a walking campaign—to walk one hundred miles in one hundred days—to raise money for prosthetics limbs for people in developing countries. Not only did she raise $16,000, she regained the mobility she lost during her pregnancies. Colleen is a writer of creative nonfiction and memoir. She has an essay in the anthology *The Spirit of a Woman* and another in *He Said What?* (Seal Press). She is currently working on a memoir about being a disabled mother. You can read about how she walks through life as an amputee at www.mymilewalk.com. Colleen lives in Bellingham, Washington, with her husband and two children, and is the program director for Big Brothers Big Sisters of Northwest Washington.

ROBYN HATCHER As owner of SpeakEtc., Robyn has helped thousands of business professionals improve their presentations, conversations, and interpersonal communication skills. In addition, Robyn is an adjunct professor at NYC's Baruch College and Fashion Institute of Technology; a trainer and curriculum developer with Leadership Transformation Group, LLC ; and a trainer/performer with Performance Plus, an innovative training and employee development program. Robyn is also a professional actress and TV and film writer. She's done radio commercials, has appeared on TV in commercials and dramas and was recently awarded Best Actress in a Short Film for her work in *Asbury Park*. She's a contributing writer to American Express Open Forum and has a book on presentation skills in development with Motivational Press. As a member of Step Up Women's Network, an organization devoted to mentoring underserved teens girls, Robyn was named April 2012 volunteer of the month.

MONICA HOLLOWAY is the author of the critically acclaimed memoir *Driving With Dead People*, described by *Newsweek* as "unforgettable," and deemed "irresistible" by *The Washington Post*. Holloway's essay from the anthology *Mommy Wars* was described by *Newsday* as "brilliant, grimly hilarious." Monica's best-selling memoir *Cowboy & Wills* was called "sweet and heartbreaking" by *People*, and was named a Mom's Choice Awards Gold Recipient. Her work can also be found in *Psychology Today*, and *Parents*. Most recently, she contributed to the anthology *Cherished*, and is presently working on her third memoir. Monica is most proud of her work as an autism advocate working at both a local and national level with the Special Needs Network (SNN) and Autism Speaks. She recently received the Women of Distinction Award from SNN in recognition for her contributions to the underserved special needs communities in Los Angeles. Monica also proudly serves on the advisory board of the National Center for Family Literacy.

LIZA LENTINI is an award-winning playwright, journalist, and author. Liza's plays have been performed around the world, including Off-Broadway's McGinn/Cazale Theatre, The Women's Project, Chicago Dramatists, and The Cherry Lane Theatre. In 2009, Manhattan Repertory Theatre performed a festival of Liza's early plays aptly titled LIZAFEST. Liza's writings have been featured in the science magazine *Discover*, men's magazine *Gear*, and the women's lifestyle magazine *Pure*, among others. In 2006, Liza founded Elephant Ensemble Theater (www.elephanttheater. com) a charitable organization, which brings educational, interactive productions to children in hospitals. In addition to designing the touring model, Liza also penned the scripts in Elephant's repertoire. Liza's proudest accomplishment, Elephant has made hundreds of sick kids smile. Learn more about Liza at www.lizalentini.com.

MEREDITH RESNICK is a right-handed, right-brain type who responds beautifully to deadlines. Her work has been published in *Newsweek, JAMA, Los Angeles Times, Santa Monica Review, Culinate, The Complete Book of Aunts* and many others, and writes the *Adoption Stories* and *More Than Caregiving* blogs at *Psychology Today*. She is the creator of *The Writer's [Inner] Journey*, a 2012 Bloggies Award finalist. A former therapist, Meredith holds a license in clinical social work, and worked in diverse settings such as inpatient psychiatry, outpatient counseling and home health/pre-hospice care. As a writer, she seeks to understand why something—or someone—turned out the way they did, and how it came to be that way. Left to her own devices, she eats too much candy. She lives in southern California with her husband and their greyhound where she is an avid creator of mosaic art on furniture. meredithresnick.com

JENNY ROUGH is a lawyer-turned-writer. Her articles and essays have appeared in a range of publications, including *AARP The Magazine, More, The Washington Post, Whole Living,* and *Yoga Journal.* She leads a RESOLVE support group for women diagnosed with infertility.

LAURENNE SALA is a storyteller, comedian, and regular contributor to The Huffington Post, KCET, and her own blog, *Humans are Funny.* With a master's degree in spiritual psychology, Laurenne teaches writing therapy workshops that encourage the sharing of human truths. She produces and hosts *Taboo Tales,* a storytelling show with the same mantra. She hates writing about herself in the third-person because she knows you know she's writing this.

MARIANNE SCHNALL is a widely published writer and interviewer. She is also the founder and executive director of Feminist.com, a leading women's website and nonprofit organization. For over sixteen years, Feminist.com has been fostering awareness, education, and activism for people all across the world. Marianne is also the cofounder of EcoMall.com, one of the oldest environmental websites promoting earth-friendly living. Marianne's writings and interviews appear at The Huffington Post, the Women's Media Center, CNN.com, and many publications, and she contributes regularly to the nationally syndicated NPR show *51% - The Women's Perspective.* Marianne was a contributor to Robin Morgan's anthology *Sisterhood is Forever: The Women's Anthology for a New Millennium.* Her latest book is *Daring to Be Ourselves: Influential Women Share Insights on Courage, Happiness and Finding Your Own Voice.* Through her writings, interviews, and websites, Marianne strives to raise awareness and inspire activism around important issues and causes.

JULIE SILVER, a celebrated and beloved performer in contemporary Jewish music, has been touring the world for the past twenty-five years, engaging audiences with her lyrical guitar playing, dynamic stage presence, and megawatt smile. With over 100,000 CDs sold, her songs have become "standards" in worship, camp, and academic settings. *It's Chanukah Time,* recorded in 2007, was the first Jewish holiday CD produced exclusively for the Barnes and Noble bookstore chain, and the only Jewish album to ever be recognized on Billboard, peaking at #5 in 2009. A life-long Red Sox fan, Julie was invited to sing the National Anthem before 38,000 fans at her beloved hometown Fenway Park. Julie speaks nationally at high schools and universities, and has become the go-to role model for people struggling to come out as gay or lesbian in the Jewish world and beyond. Julie lives in Southern California with her partner, television producer Mary Connelly, and their two delicious daughters, Sarah and Catherine. www.juliesilver.com

TERESA STACK was born in Ohio and raised in the fabulous (and underrated) town of Pittsburgh, Pennsylvania. After attending Penn State, where she learned basic human socialization skills, she moved to NYC, landing a job as a receptionist for some fashion magazines. There she was expertly and generously mentored by a series of awesome women (and some pretty awesome men) and just a few years later managed the circulation department for Fairchild Publications' fourteen magazines. For the past fifteen years, she has worked as president of *The Nation,* happily trading fashion for progressive politics, and trying in turn to mentor (and get out of the way of) a talented group of precocious female (and male) lefties who still believe in making the world a better place. She splits her time between NY and Pennsylvania, enjoying many hobbies, volunteering, and walking in the woods with her all-around-excellent husband and their two rescue dogs.

LYENA STRELKOFF is a performer, writer, speaker, and coach. Her critically acclaimed, autobiographical one-woman play, *Caterpillar Soup,* has been touring throughout the United States since 2007. She regularly speaks to university students, health care professionals and civic groups about her disability experience and the transformative power of loss. She is also a business and life coach, helping people claim their stories to create joyous, thriving careers and lives. Her blog, *It's Not About the Chair* (http://itsnotaboutthechair.com), shares wisdom and humor culled from her daily life. She lives in Los Angeles with her husband, son, service dog, wheelchair, and all the chaos that ensues.

TRACY J. THOMAS is a professional documentary photographer, freelance writer, blogger and website designer located in Northern, California. She is also a general partner for the online op-ed website the iPinion Syndicate, and serves as Multimedia Director and Photography Editor. Her work has been featured in numerous publications and websites. She has been a featured artist for the *Mobile Photography Awards*; *Pixels: The Art of the iPhone;* and *iPhoneArt* websites and has been exhibited in local and international art galleries. Tracy was the 2010 recipient of the "View of Farmlands" grant commission through the Yolo County Arts Council and the James Irvine Foundation. She received her M.F.A. in Documentary Photography from the Academy of Art University, San Francisco and her M.A. in Sports Management from the University of San Francisco. Website: www.tracyjthomasphotography.com, Blog: www.tracyjthomasphotography.wordpress.com

KRISTINE VAN RADEN stumbled upon a miracle fifteen years ago with her best friend, Molly Davis. A shared idea led to an interesting project, which led to a dinner party with a slightly inebriated and highly enthusiastic publisher. Soon Kristine and Molly were interviewing strangers on street corners, in produce sections of grocery stores—even on an elevator trip up the Eiffel Tower—compiling a collection of letters from women around the world that became *Letters to Our Daughters.* Since then, they formed *Matters That Matter,* offering workshops around the country, building upon the honesty and transparency of the women they have met throughout this experience. They have come to understand that we are all more alike than we are different, and that if we can get past the differences, there are common threads that connect us as human beings.

KATE VAN RADEN is a self-taught photographer who pens both a fashion blog and poetry blog: www.katevanraden.wordpress.com. She is also a twenty-seven-year-old woman who has struggled with the trials and tribulations of anorexia for the better part of five years throughout college and modeling in New York. She is currently juggling a zoology degree, a full-time job, and her continued pursuit of wellness. Kate continues to attend treatment and therapy for her mental illness; making great strides towards increasing personal capabilities for love, growth, and self-acceptance. All the while, she remains passionately and vigorously committed to her work with endangered species. Kate lives with her three-year old hedgehog, Rosebud, in an apartment in Portland, Oregon.

KEDREN WERNER was born and raised, and continues to live in Los Angeles, California. She has been married for twenty years and has a fourteen-year-old son. She is a published writer (personal essays). This is her first piece in an anthology.

AMY WISE is the author of: *Believe in Yourself ~ Inspire Others ~ Spread Joy*, and her work appears in the anthology *Oil and Water and Other Things That Don't Mix*. She created *The Many Shades of Love* blog (www.themanyshadesoflove.blogspot.com), and is a contributing writer for *EmbraceUS Multicultural Magazine*, *TheNextFamily. com*, and the *Oil and Water* blog. Amy is a guest writer for various websites, blogs, and newspapers, and is a ghostwriter and editor for all genres of writers. She recently edited *The Eat From Home Diet: How to Get a Slim Body and Fat Wallet*. She is currently writing a memoir and working on a screenplay. She lives in San Diego with her husband, Jamie, and daughter, Tatiana. www.amywisewriter.com

MARCIA G. YERMAN is a writer, activist, artist, and curator based in New York City. Her articles—profiles, interviews, reporting, and essays—focus on women's issues, human rights, culture, and the arts. She is a contributing writer for *EmpowHER* and *Women News Network*. She has been published at *Huffington Post*, *AlterNet*, *The Women's Media Center*, *Daily Kos*, and *The Raw Story*, among others. Her articles are archived at www.mgyerman.com. Her artwork is online at http://marciagyerman.com. Marcia is the cofounder of cultureID, a 501(c)(3) for those in the cultural arena doing work with political/social intent and content. cultureID connects nonprofit organizations and creatives to amplify a full range of global issues. Marcia continually promotes the view that if women's frame of reference is not reflected in the arts (literature, film, theater, visual arts), then their true identities and visions will be defined by male-driven popular culture. Find her on Twitter @mgyerman.

VICTORIA ZACKHEIM wrote *The Bone Weaver* (novel) and edited five anthologies: *The Other Woman: 21 Wives, Lovers, and Others Talk Openly About Sex, Deception, Love, and Betrayal; For Keeps: Women Tell the Truth About Their Bodies, Growing Older, and Acceptance; The Face in the Mirror: Writers Reflect on Their Dreams of Youth and the Reality of Age; He Said What? Women Write About the Moments When Everything Changed;* and *Exit Laughing: How Humor Takes the Sting Out of Death.* Victoria adapted essays from *The Other Woman* and created a play scheduled for development and production with The Berkeley Repertory Theatre. She wrote the documentary, *Where Birds Never Sang: The Story of Ravensbrück and Sachsenhausen Concentration Camps* (On the Road Productions), and *Maidstone*, a screenplay in development (No Attachment Films and Identity Films). She teaches Personal Essay in the UCLA Extension Writers' Program and is a 2010 San Francisco Library Laureate.

SELECTED TITLES FROM *Seal Press*

For more than thirty years, Seal Press has published groundbreaking books. By women. For women.

Drinking Diaries: Women Serve Their Stories Straight Up, edited by Caren Osten Gerszberg and Leah Odze Epstein. $15.00, 978-1-58005-411-9. Celebrated writers take a candid look at the pleasures and pains of drinking, and the many ways in which it touches women's lives.

Marrying George Clooney: Confessions from a Midlife Crisis, by Amy Ferris. $16.95, 978-1-58005-297-9. In this candid look at menopause, Amy Ferris chronicles every one of her funny, sad, hysterical, down and dirty, and raw to the bones insomnia-fueled stories.

Pale Girl Speaks: A Year Uncovered, by Hillary Fogelson. $16.00, 978-1-58005-444-7. An edgy, funny memoir about a woman who became angry and self-absorbed when she was diagnosed with melanoma—until her father was diagnosed with the same skin cancer, and she had to learn to lead by example and let go of her fear.

Licking the Spoon: A Memoir of Food, Family, and Identity, by Candace Walsh. $16.00, 978-1-58005-391-4. The story of how—accompanied by pivotal recipes, cookbooks, culinary movements, and guides—one woman learned that you cannot only recover but blossom after a comically horrible childhood if you just have the right recipes, a little luck, and an appetite for life's next meal.

We Hope You Like This Song: An Overly Honest Story about Friendship, Death, and Mix Tapes, by Bree Housley. $16.00, 978-1-58005-431-7. Bree Housley's sweet, quirky, and hilarious tribute to her lifelong friend, and her chronicle of how she honored her after her premature death.

She Bets Her Life: The True Story of a Gambling Addict and the Women Who Saved Her Life, by Mary Sojourner. $17.95, 978-1-58005-298-6. One woman's account of her personal struggle with gambling addiction, this is a hard-hitting confession of the journey to the bottom—and back up.

Find Seal Press Online
www.SealPress.com
www.Facebook.com/SealPress
Twitter: @SealPress